Manipulation

What People High in Dark Triad Traits Know About Human Psychology, How to Analyze People, Persuasion, and Mind Control

Contents

PART 1: MANIPULATION 1

INTRODUCTION 2

CHAPTER ONE: THE NINE DARK PERSONALITY TRAITS 4

CHAPTER TWO: THE DARK TRIAD 23

CHAPTER THREE: NARCISSISM 27

CHAPTER FOUR: PSYCHOPATHY 35

CHAPTER FIVE: MACHIAVELLIANISM 44

CHAPTER SIX: SADISM 51

CHAPTER SEVEN: GASLIGHTERS AND EMOTIONAL
MANIPULATION 59

CHAPTER EIGHT: HOW TO DETECT A LIE THROUGH BODY
LANGUAGE 68

CHAPTER NINE: DEALING WITH WORKSPACE MANIPULATORS .. 72

CHAPTER TEN: HOW NLP IS LEVERAGED TO MANIPULATE
OTHERS 76

CHAPTER ELEVEN: MIND CONTROL AND BRAIN WASHING 81

CHAPTER TWELVE: MEDIA MANIPULATION AND SUBLIMINAL
INFLUENCING 88

CHAPTER THIRTEEN: THE DARK PSYCHOLOGY OF CYBERSPACE 92

CHAPTER FOURTEEN: THE DARK PSYCHOLOGY OF CULTS 96

CHAPTER FIFTEEN: EXAMPLES OF POLITICAL PROPAGANDA 99

CHAPTER SIXTEEN: HOW TO PROTECT YOURSELF FROM
MANIPULATORS 105

CONCLUSION 109

PART 2: HOW TO ANALYZE PEOPLE 110

INTRODUCTION 111

CHAPTER ONE: THE BENEFITS OF ANALYZING OTHERS 113

How Psychologists Analyze You 113

One-Tenth of a Second 116

Why You Should Learn to Read People 116

CHAPTER TWO: UNDERSTANDING HUMAN BEHAVIOR &
PSYCHOLOGY 120

The Psychologist's Definition of Attitude 120

Behavior Analysis 121

Techniques for Behavior Analysis 122

Your Brain and Your Behavior 122

Other Factors that Affect Human Behavior 124

The Three Laws of Human Behavior 125

Techniques Used by Behavioral Psychologists 126

CHAPTER THREE: THE 16 PERSONALITY TYPES 130

The Myers-Briggs Personality Types 130

Tips for Identifying Each Type 137

CHAPTER FOUR: THE SECRETS OF SPEED READING 140

Breaking Down the Categories of Myers' Briggs 140

Speed Reading People 142

Common Mistakes When Reading People 145

CHAPTER FIVE: HOW TO READ BODY LANGUAGE 146

Why Nonverbal Communication Matters 147

Forms of Nonverbal Communication 147

Reading Body Language 149

More Tips for Reading Nonverbal Communication 151

CHAPTER SIX: HOW TO ANALYZE HANDWRITING 153

Things to Keep in Mind about Graphology 153

Another Way to Analyze Handwriting 155

Forensic Document Analysis in Practice 156

Fun Graphology Facts 157

Why Reading Handwriting is a Useful Skill 160

CHAPTER SEVEN: MIND-READING WITH NEURO-LINGUISTIC PROGRAMMING 162

NLP IN ACTION 162

NLP MIND READING 163

HOW TO MIND READ 163

HOW CAN YOU READ PEOPLE'S MINDS? 164

PRACTICE ACCESSING CUES 165

WHO USES NLP? 165

HYPNOTIC MIND READING TECHNIQUES 166

CHAPTER EIGHT: DARK PSYCHOLOGY – RECOGNIZING THE DARK TRIAD 170

HOW TO SPOT YOUR NEIGHBORHOOD NARCISSIST 171

HOW TO SPOT YOUR MASTER MACHIAVELLIAN 173

HOW TO SPOT YOUR SADISTIC PSYCHOPATH 174

CHAPTER NINE: SIGNS OF LIES AND DECEPTION 179

THE VOICE BEHIND THE WORDS 182

TIPS FOR SPOTTING LIARS 183

NO UNIVERSAL SIGN FOR LIES 187

CHAPTER TEN: SPOTTING FLIRTERS AND SEDUCERS 188

LET'S PLAY "SPOT THE FLIRT" 188

THREE STEPS TO SUCCESSFUL FLIRTING 191

CHAPTER ELEVEN: IDENTIFYING MASS MANIPULATION AND PROPAGANDA 194

MEDIA MANIPULATION TACTICS 194

SOCIAL MEDIA MANIPULATES YOU TOO 198

TIPS FOR DEALING WITH SOCIAL MEDIA 198

HOW DEEP THE RABBIT HOLE GOES 199

22 PROPAGANDA TECHNIQUES YOU SHOULD KNOW 201

CHAPTER TWELVE: TRAINING YOUR ANALYTICAL MIND DAILY 205

WHY ANALYTICAL THINKING SKILLS MATTER 205

SEVEN STEPS TO BETTER ANALYTICAL THINKING 206

Part 1: Manipulation

The Little-Known Secrets People High in Dark Triad Traits Know About Persuasion, Human Psychology, Analyzing Body Language, and Mind Control

THE LITTLE-KNOWN SECRETS
People High in Dark Triad Traits know About Persuasion, Human Psychology, Analyzing Body Language, and Mind Control

NEIL MORTON

Introduction

Today's world is a hub of influence—people are continually finding a way to get others to do their bidding. Everyone has an ulterior motive, and if you are not careful, you will get pulled into the sunken place where your subconsciousness becomes a plaything for evil people. From social media influencers and public speakers to your boss, coworker, friend, family, and companion—so many people might try to influence you.

At first, the idea may seem mostly harmless. However, do you know the point in which influence becomes manipulation? How do you tell the difference between positive or negative influence and manipulations? Not a lot of people can answer this question, and that is all right. But there is no reason why you should not educate yourself, especially with the amount of manipulation, mind control, and brainwashing techniques that thrive in personal, professional, and social relationships.

This book is for people who want to learn the secret strategies, tips, and techniques used by manipulators to influence and possibly overthrow the very foundation of their victims' identities, precisely to use the information to protect themselves. If you fall under this category of people, read on.

For centuries, certain elements in society have used the art of manipulation to gain, exert, and maintain control and dominance over others. Based on years of research, scientists have established that the people who do this the most are people with the *Dark Triad* personality traits. *What are the dark triad traits? And who exhibits them?* These questions and more are answered in this incredible guide.

The book begins by talking about *Personality Psychology* and how—much like everything—psychology has a dark side. It then progresses to the people who embrace the dark aspect of psychology and the techniques they use to achieve control over other people's minds and lives.

From beginning to end, this guide covers everything you need to know about manipulation. You will learn about mind control techniques, body language, and the use of human psychology. More importantly, you will find out how the government and media influence your behavior without realizing it.

So, without further ado, it is time to dissect the art of manipulation . . .

Chapter One: The Nine Dark Personality Traits

According to the American Psychological Association (APA), psychology is the scientific study of the mind and behavior. Psychology is multifaceted and encompasses several aspects of the study, one of which is personality psychology. Humans have been interested in understanding personality right from the beginning of time. In ancient China, personality traits were assigned based on the birth year of the individuals. Those who study the stars believe that human nature is defined by the planet's position on the day a person is born concerning other celestial items and objects. The Greek physician Hippocrates believed that bodily fluids characterized personality was. At the same time, some other Greeks thought that it was founded on a specific disease. Throughout history, humans have found personality intriguing, and they have persistently tried to understand it. Science also has much say about personality and personality development.

How does science explain the dominant characteristics of individuals? Well, that is precisely what personality psychology entails. This branch of psychology is dedicated entirely to the "nature vs. nurture" argument, which is devoted to understanding how human behavior is formed.

Personality is an interesting term that you, like everyone else, are familiar with, but find it difficult to describe or define. At one point in your life, you must have made a statement about liking someone's personality. Phrases like, "I love his personality" or "I love her personality" are things that we have said or heard. You are probably familiar with "personality disorder" too. But if someone asked you to give them a few synonyms for personality right now, would you be able to? Like many people, you may come up with just a few words that fit. This is normal, as personality is an abstract concept. You cannot wholly describe it with a single word or phrase. Still, it is essential to grasp the definitions and examples if you want to understand human behavior and personality psychology. Knowing how the multiple aspects of an individual come together to become a "whole" will help you advance in life.

Personality originates from the Latin word *persona*, which means mask. In olden times, a persona was a mask worn on stage by actors to conceal their actual identities while portraying a particular character trait. According to the APA, personality is "individual differences in characteristic patterns of thinking, feeling, and behaving." Personality is who you are, from how you think and behave to how you live your life and form relationships with others. Your character is unique to you. It is a set of characteristics that informs how you react to your thoughts, emotions, motivations, people, and your environment at large. You may also think of your personality as your own unique pattern of thoughts, feelings, and behaviors, which, to a significant extent, influences your values, attitude, and self-perception. Some of the best synonyms for personality are character, nature, temperament, disposition, identity, etc. Still, these words do not fully capture the essence of what personality is.

Personality is an intriguing subject, and this is evident in the many fun facts on personality and personality types. For example, science suggests that personality can be affected by birth order. This means that first, middle, last, and only children usually are alike in some ways, regardless of the family they come from. This explains why people say that first-born children act a certain way or that only children are usually treated one way or another. Another exciting personality fact is that falling or being in love with another person can modify your personality-reducing neurotic dispositions, including getting annoyed or worried. Also, your personality changes the older you get, which is why people become nicer as they age. Have you ever had your parent tell you that, "You should have met your grandma twenty years back?" Did you also know that some foods are connected with personality disorders? So, if you eat specific kinds of food more, you will likely develop a personality disorder. Isn't that interesting? Finally, scientists say that optimistic individuals tend to live longer because positive thinking results in a healthier and inadvertently longer life. You could go on and on about personality, and there will always be one fact to blow your mind and reinforce the belief that it is an exciting topic.

Because you are the one person who knows yourself best, you might describe your personality. However, have you ever wondered what the scientific study of personality is all about? Personality psychology is defined as "a scientific study that aims to show how people are individually different due to psychology forces." This means that personality psychology aims to understand how thinking and behavior can vary from individual to individual. The purpose of personality psychology is to help you know how you develop that set of peculiar characteristics to you and how it influences your thinking and behavior. Personality psychologists examine the variation in personality among individuals, as well as the similarities. This is how they can identify personality disorders in people. Understanding your nature and that of the people around you gives valuable insight into your mental and emotional wellbeing. More often than not, some people are taken advantage of by people with certain personalities, but they never realize it.

Several factors contribute to the development of the individual you are today, including life experiences, upbringing, and genetics. Most people argue that the one thing that really separates you from others is the pattern of thoughts, feelings, and behaviors that constitute your personality. There is no consensus on a specific singular definition of personality. Still, many professionals agree that it formulates from within every individual and rarely ever changes throughout life. Understanding personality helps you predict how people around you will respond to specific situations and the things they value the most. Knowing about the most widely-accepted personality theories and their history throughout time can go a long way to understanding how psychology researchers study personality psychology. Although some of the arguments are considered silly by many people, it is indisputable that each theory adds something to the puzzle about personality psychology. Every personality psychology theory explains what humans' inner and outer personas comprise of. An interesting thing to note about the scientific study of personality is that what you believe you know about your personality is not in line with scientific research.

Over the years, numerous theories have arisen to explain and break down the many aspects of personality. Some approaches focus on how personality develops, while others deal with differences in personality among people.

Galen's Theory is one of the foremost personality theories. It is built on Hippocrates' beliefs and notions about personality. Galen, a Greek physician, writer, and philosopher, alleged that a balanced temperament equates health. Hence, you are automatically healthy if your temperament is stable. Otherwise, your bodily fluids are out of sync. The fluids were referred to as sanguine, melancholy, choleric, and phlegmatic. Galen's description of personality originated from the four elements: earth, water, wind, and fire. For more than 1,000 years, Galen's personality theory was the widely-accepted theory. Although this theory has been proven to be false as human civilization evolved, it is intriguing to know that humans and researchers have been interested in understanding the human psyche as far back as 2000 BC. This theory was expanded further by Immanuel Kant in the eighteenth century.

Another popular theory is Gall's theory of personality, which was proposed in the 1700s by Franz Gall, a German physician. The Gall theory is skull-based and is also referred to as phrenology. According to the physician, measuring the length of the area between the bumps on an individual's head can reveal the size of their brain, as well as information about their personality. You could find out how kind and affable a person is and whether they could commit murder. Eventually, this theory was ruled a pseudoscience by researchers, but it was popular and accepted for several years.

There are also Freud and Erikson's theories—originally developed by Freud and subsequently expanded on by Erik Erikson. Sigmund Freud is known as the founder of one of the most widely-known personality theories. His psychoanalytic theory lays out a series of phases and internal conflicts that humans undergo before their personality is formed. Later, Erikson also built a comparable argument based on the work of Freud. Although there are significant differences in the two theories, both agree that early childhood experiences and phases influence personality formation. In other words, the events that happen to you as you go from child to adolescent to adult have a significant effect on whom you become.

In this day and age, the most influential is the Trait Personality Theories. Theories under this category are premised on the belief that personality is made up of broad traits and dispositions. Several approaches have emerged to identify the specific attributes that serve as vital aspects of personality and evaluate the total number of personality traits. The very first psychologist to describe personality regarding individual characteristics was Gordon Allport. From his perspective, Allport argued that there are three varying kinds of traits: common, central, and cardinal. Common traits are those shared by people within a particular culture, central traits are those that comprise a person's personality, and cardinal traits are the dominant traits that an individual becomes primarily known for. Therefore, your cardinal traits are what you exhibit the most, which is what most people would describe you with. For example, Jesus was widely known for forgiveness. He was forgiving, so much so that he laid his life down for other people to attain forgiveness. That is an instance of a cardinal trait. Allport further suggested that people have as many as 4,000 traits.

Another psychologist, Raymond Cattell, argued that there are only sixteen individual traits. He further suggested that these traits exist as a pattern and that people possess them in varying degrees.

Yet another psychologist, Hans Eysenck, further narrowed the list made by Cartell to extroversion, psychoticism, and neuroticism.

However, the most popular trait theory of personality is the Big Five theory, which is widely accepted by professionals. Many researchers and psychologists concur with this theory. The Big Five theory proposes that personality comprises five comprehensive personality dimensions:

- Agreeableness
- Conscientiousness
- Extroversion
- Neuroticism
- Openness

However, the "Big Five" theory or trait theories are not based on the work of a sole researcher; it was created based on research and studies by many scholars.

The theory further explains that each of the individual traits exists on a wide spectrum. Your personality lies somewhere in the spectrum for each stated trait. This means that these five traits aren't an "either-or" thing. They are more like a gauge, where you can fall on the high end or low end. For instance, you may be high in agreeableness and extroversion, but be somewhat low for openness, neuroticism, and conscientiousness. People who fall on the high end of openness are usually very creative, emotional, intellectual, liberal, progressive, and love to take risks and go on daring adventures.

On the contrary, individuals who are low in openness tend to dislike change and are resistant to creative or new ideas. People with high agreeableness tend to care more about others and are willingly help people in need. They are also empathetic and inclined to take a great interest in what others are going through. Those on the bottom end of the spectrum, on the other hand, are usually manipulative, selfish, and competitive.

Highly neurotic individuals are prone to experiencing anxiety, stress, mood swings, and worry. People on the lower end rarely get depressed and are generally stable emotionally, while those on the upper end of the extroversion spectrum enjoy meeting new friends and being the center of admiration and attention. They are also very energized around people and do not like to be by themselves. Furthermore, they rarely think before speaking and tend to be talkative.

Individuals that are not extroverted find social gatherings tiring, like to be alone, and find "small talk" unnecessary.

Conscientious people love to keep things in order, have astonishing self-control, value timeliness, and set and meet deadlines.

Those on the lower end of the conscientiousness scale are the people who "go with the flow," do things on impulse, and procrastinate.

After a considerable amount of research, experts who focused on personality psychology found that the five traits listed above are:

- Universal
- Biological

Although the traits may increase or decrease as you age, they stay pretty much the same in adulthood.

As interesting and seemingly positive as personality psychology is, it also has a dark side. Regardless of where you live, you must have met one or more "bad" people. In fact, you have probably met more bad people than good. What makes these people bad? Their personality? When people talk about psychology, they mostly talk about the positive and beneficial aspects. Countless books that explain how you can use practices like *mindfulness* to influence your thoughts and behaviors; however, a lot of people do not realize that psychology can also be used in ways that are not so beneficial. It is important to note that humans are sometimes not in control of their actions, but they often believe they are. Therefore, you may be exhibiting a behavioral pattern that falls on the dark side of psychology without realizing it.

Dark psychology can be regarded as both a mental construct and the study of humans' psychological inclination to take advantage of others, based on certain psychological, psychopathic, and psychopathological drives. The tendency to prey upon others is common to all humans, but the drive is stronger in some people. While many of the human population generally restrain themselves from acting on these selfish and pathological tendencies, many people act on them. The study of dark psychology is based on these people who cannot or do not want to train their impulses and refrain from acting on their deepest desires. History and everyday life are full of examples of people who act ruthlessly, selfishly, and malevolently. Dark psychology aims to understand the thoughts, feelings, perceptions, and motivations that build up to predatory behaviors in many people.

Psychology experts have assigned different names to the dark tendencies in humans. Under an umbrella term, these tendencies are referred to as the dark traits. There are nine, but most people know of one (Narcissism) because of its popularity and misconception in mainstream media. The nine dark personality traits are:

- Egoism
- Machiavellianism
- Moral disengagement
- Narcissism
- Psychological entitlement
- Psychopathy
- Sadism
- Self-interest
- Spitefulness

These nine traits form what is regarded as the dark personality core. However, Psychopathy, Machiavellianism, and Narcissism are regarded as the darkest of the nine traits, and together, they make up what is known as the Dark Triad. Before the dark triad is discussed in-depth, here is a brief breakdown of the nine traits and why they form the core of dark personality psychology.

Egoism is described as excessive absorption or preoccupation with one's achievement at the disadvantage of others. Egoists believe that self-interest should always be put above all else, regardless of whose interest is at stake.

Machiavellianism is the belief that the ends justify the means. Machiavellians behave in a manipulative and callous way, without caring about who gets hurt in the process of getting what they want.

Moral disengagement is a cognitive processing style that enables people to behave unethically without feeling distressed. People who are morally disengaged can hurt others without feeling bad about it.

Narcissism is excessive absorption with oneself, a belief that one is superior to others, and an unreasonable need for attention and admiration. Narcissists believe they have more to offer in life than others.

Psychological entitlement is the belief that one is superior to other people for no apparent reason. Psychologically-entitled people tend to believe that they deserve better in life than others.

Psychopathy refers to a lack of empathy and self-control and a tendency to act on impulse. Psychopathic people are rarely able to control their actions, and they feel no remorse for how they treat other people. Most serial killers are psychopathic.

Sadism is an innate desire to inflict physical, mental or emotional harm on others for one's pleasure or benefit. Sadists gain immeasurable joy from torturing or causing harm to others.

Self-interest is the desire to advance one's financial or social status, regardless of obstacles.

Spitefulness is the willingness or eagerness to hurt others—even if one gets hurt in the process.

These nine dark traits have something in common, and the common factor is referred to as "D-factor" by personality psychology experts. The next chapter specifically talks about the malevolent Dark Triad and the D-factor. Your takeaway here should be that psychology is not all positive and rosy—as many people are made to believe via the mainstream media. There is a dark side of psychology, and it is very important to understand it. No matter what you do, some malevolent people put themselves before all. They will hurt you—emotionally, mentally, physically, financially, and sexually—unless you learn their tactics and how to steer clear of them.

Dark Core of Personality Test

It is vital to note that while some people use the dark tactics of mind control—which are associated with the dark traits—many use them without realizing it. Most people do not manipulate with intent, but, of course, those who do it intentionally are the ones that most books address. Those who are unaware of using the tactics have either learned the behaviors in childhood, either from their parents or guardians, in their adolescent years, or not until adulthood. This kind of person learns the behavior by happenstance. For example, if you intentionally use a manipulation tactic on someone you know, and it gets you what you want, you are likely to keep using the tactic for that same person—but you won't fully realize the damage that you are doing to them. In certain cases, some people even receive coaching on dark tactics, such as training programs in sales and marketing.

To ascertain whether you are subconsciously using dark psychology, take the test below.

1. I am the life of the party
- o Disagree
- o Slightly Disagree
- o Neutral
- o Slightly Agree

o Agree

2. I have no reason to feel concern for others

o Disagree

o Slightly Disagree

o Neutral

o Slightly Agree

o Agree

3. I am prepared at all times

o Disagree

o Slightly Disagree

o Neutral

o Slightly Agree

o Agree

4. I am easily stressed out

o Disagree

o Slightly Disagree

o Neutral

o Slightly Agree

o Agree

5. I have an impeccable command of language

o Disagree

o Slightly Disagree

o Neutral

o Slightly Agree

o Agree

6. I rarely talk

o Disagree

o Slightly Disagree

o Neutral

o Slightly Agree

o Agree

7. I am interested in people

o Disagree

o Slightly Disagree

- o Neutral
- o Slightly Agree
- o Agree

8. I leave my possessions with people
- o Disagree
- o Slightly Disagree
- o Neutral
- o Slightly Agree
- o Agree

9. I am always relaxed
- o Disagree
- o Slightly Disagree
- o Neutral
- o Slightly Agree
- o Agree

10. I find it difficult to grasp abstract concepts
- o Disagree
- o Slightly Disagree
- o Neutral
- o Slightly Agree
- o Agree

11. I feel unrelaxed around people
- o Disagree
- o Slightly Disagree
- o Neutral
- o Slightly Agree
- o Agree

12. I enjoy taunting people
- o Disagree
- o Slightly Disagree
- o Neutral
- o Slightly Agree
- o Agree

13. I am attentive to details

- o Disagree
- o Slightly Disagree
- o Neutral
- o Slightly Agree
- o Agree

14. I worry a lot

- o Disagree
- o Slightly Disagree
- o Neutral
- o Slightly Agree
- o Agree

15. I have an explicit imagination

- o Disagree
- o Slightly Disagree
- o Neutral
- o Slightly Agree
- o Agree

16. I prefer to stay away in the background

- o Disagree
- o Slightly Disagree
- o Neutral
- o Slightly Agree
- o Agree

17. I put myself in others' shoes

- o Disagree
- o Slightly Disagree
- o Neutral
- o Slightly Agree
- o Agree

18. I am unorganized

- o Disagree
- o Slightly Disagree
- o Neutral

o Slightly Agree

o Agree

19. I rarely feel blue

o Disagree

o Slightly Disagree

o Neutral

o Slightly Agree

o Agree

20. Abstract ideas bore me

o Disagree

o Slightly Disagree

o Neutral

o Slightly Agree

o Agree

21. I am nice to people

o Disagree

o Slightly Disagree

o Neutral

o Slightly Agree

o Agree

22. I like to start conversations

o Disagree

o Slightly Disagree

o Neutral

o Slightly Agree

o Agree

23. I have no interest in people's problems

o Disagree

o Slightly Disagree

o Neutral

o Slightly Agree

o Agree

24. I do things meticulously
- o Disagree
- o Slightly Disagree
- o Neutral
- o Slightly Agree
- o Agree

25. I don't waste time
- o Disagree
- o Slightly Disagree
- o Neutral
- o Slightly Agree
- o Agree

26. I get disturbed easily
- o Disagree
- o Slightly Disagree
- o Neutral
- o Slightly Agree
- o Agree

27. I have great ideas
- o Disagree
- o Slightly Disagree
- o Neutral
- o Slightly Agree
- o Agree

28. I have very little to contribute
- o Disagree
- o Slightly Disagree
- o Neutral
- o Slightly Agree
- o Agree

29. I forget to return things to their place properly
- o Disagree
- o Slightly Disagree
- o Neutral

- o Slightly Agree
- o Agree

30. I am easily upset
- o Disagree
- o Slightly Disagree
- o Neutral
- o Slightly Agree
- o Agree

31. I am not good with imagination
- o Disagree
- o Slightly Disagree
- o Neutral
- o Slightly Agree
- o Agree

32. I talk to different people when I am at a party
- o Disagree
- o Slightly Disagree
- o Neutral
- o Slightly Agree
- o Agree

33. I have no interest in what people say
- o Disagree
- o Slightly Disagree
- o Neutral
- o Slightly Agree
- o Agree

34. I like being organized
- o Disagree
- o Slightly Disagree
- o Neutral
- o Slightly Agree
- o Agree

35. I experience mood changes a lot
- o Disagree
- o Slightly Disagree
- o Neutral
- o Slightly Agree
- o Agree

36. I understand things quickly
- o Disagree
- o Slightly Disagree
- o Neutral
- o Slightly Agree
- o Agree

37. I believe people don't care about one another
- o Disagree
- o Slightly Disagree
- o Neutral
- o Slightly Agree
- o Agree

38. I believe lies can help me get ahead
- o Disagree
- o Slightly Disagree
- o Neutral
- o Slightly Agree
- o Agree

39. I believe everyone would hurt each other if they had the chance
- o Disagree
- o Slightly Disagree
- o Neutral
- o Slightly Agree
- o Agree

40. I believe people who share their secrets are unwise
- o Disagree
- o Slightly Disagree

o Neutral

o Slightly Agree

o Agree

41. I am more deserving than others

o Disagree

o Slightly Disagree

o Neutral

o Slightly Agree

o Agree

42. I deserve a better life than I currently have

o Disagree

o Slightly Disagree

o Neutral

o Slightly Agree

o Agree

43. I imagine having extraordinary prestige

o Disagree

o Slightly Disagree

o Neutral

o Slightly Agree

o Agree

44. People think I'm extremely worthy of adoration

o Disagree

o Slightly Disagree

o Neutral

o Slightly Agree

o Agree

45. Stupid people deserve whatever comes their way

o Disagree

o Slightly Disagree

o Neutral

o Slightly Agree

o Agree

Chapter Two: The Dark Triad

For years, psychologists have tried to understand the traits that push people to commit socially unacceptable, offensive, and sometimes criminal acts. In the quest to better understand dark behaviors, the term *Dark Triad* became known by many. The dark triad may seem like a term from your favorite thriller movie about assassins, but that is not how psychology explains it. The term, which is now widely popular, was coined by Paulhus and Williams in 2002 to describe the three darkest personality traits that are unusually malevolent: narcissism, Machiavellianism, and psychopathy. Recently, researchers argue that "sadism" should be added to the dark triad due to its similarities with other conditions. Sadism, as published by the *European Journal of Psychological Assessment*, meets the criteria found in narcissism, psychopathy, and Machiavellianism, while bringing a new element that is foreign to the other dark traits—an intrinsic feeling of pleasure derived from hurting others.

In recent years, there have been increasing reports about people getting defrauded by cyber hackers and posers. They commit their fraudulent acts without a single atom of remorse. These are examples of people with dark triad traits. Throughout history, there are also examples of people who have maliciously put their interest above all others, which shows that dark triad traits have probably been around since the dawn of humanity. You may have met people like this in your school or workplace. Or you may even have some of these traits without knowing it. One thing about people with dark traits is that they are usually aware that they are doing something hurtful to others. Still, most do not feel bad about it. They don't feel bad, because they have an impaired sense of empathy. Some even lack empathy altogether.

On first examination, you may believe there are differences between the three traits that form the dark triad. Some people believe that it is much better to be a narcissist than a psychopath. Some people even proudly say things like, "I'm a narcissist. I just can't help it." However, the truth is that these three traits, and the other six traits, all have precariously close links. Psychopaths are mostly narcissists, even though all narcissists may not be psychopaths. All the dark traits stem from the same tendency. Basically, this means that most dark traits are manifested from a singular disposition common to all: the dark core of personality. Practically, what this means is that people who have the tendencies to portray any of these dark traits are also strongly likely to show one or more of the other eight traits. That is, if you are a narcissist, you have a strong tendency to be a psychopath, sadist, or both.

Researchers from the University of Copenhagen surveyed more than 2,500 people. They found a commonality between each of the dark personality traits portrayed by the people they surveyed. Based on their research, the D-factor is the common denominator present in all dark traits, particularly the dark triad. The dark core of personality, otherwise known as the D-factor, is "the general disposition to maximize one's individual utility—disregarding, accepting, or malevolently provoking disutility for others—accompanied by beliefs that serve as justifications." Simply put, all dark traits go back to the underlying human tendency of putting one's interests and goals over others' needs, interests, and goals. Most times, to the extent of gaining pleasure from others' distress—

accompanied by different beliefs and perceptions that are used to justify the actions, thus preventing the feelings of guilt, regret, shame, and the like that should naturally be elicited in situations like that. So, people who have one or more of these traits do whatever it takes to get what they want, even if it means hurting other people.

Now, here is the thing: even though the dark traits generally originate from that common core, the aspects are predominantly different in each trait. For example, a justification for reprehensible actions is predominant in narcissism. In contrast, sadism is predominantly ruled by the provocation of disutility for others. Therefore, while narcissists will mostly do things and find ways to justify their actions, sadists intentionally find ways to make others suffer. From a narcissistic boss to entitled clients and selfish partners, the one common denominator is that they all prioritize their needs and personal gain over yours. When you put your individual gain above everything else, you will find justifications for inflicting harm on others in the process, and you can avoid experiencing the normal feelings of guilt and shame.

If you know someone who puts their personal ambition above everything else, they certainly have one or more dark personality traits. A person who shows one of these malevolent behaviors has an increased likelihood of engaging in other malevolent behaviors. If your boss acts like an egomaniac today, they have a strong tendency to feel and act morally superior tomorrow. The D-factor can be used to evaluate the possibility that an individual who has been offensive before will engage in more offensive or harmful behaviors. Therefore, once you identify one of the nine dark traits in a partner, coworker, or client, it should be all the red flag that you need to start avoiding them. If you do not avoid them as soon as you figure that out, they may end up getting you entangled in their web. Soon, it will become a cycle that you may not escape from.

From each trait's description in the previous chapter, it is easy to see the common core in all nine. However, each of the dark triads—

25

including sadism—will be detailed further, and how the dark core of personality plays out in each one.

Chapter Three: Narcissism

Narcissism is more prominent in the population than you might realize. Generally, "narcissist" refers to people who are obnoxious and full of themselves, but the term is much more than that. A narcissistic personality disorder is diagnosed to people who have an uncontrollable level of narcissistic traits. However, this book is not looking at the clinical aspect of narcissism.

Many people believe that narcissism is growing rapidly worldwide, particularly among the younger generations, but psychological research begs to differ. Psychologists view narcissism on a spectrum. This particular dark trait is spread throughout the population, with the majority falling in the middle and a few at either of the spectrum's extreme ends.

Narcissism is most commonly measured and evaluated using the Narcissistic Personality Inventory, which was developed in 1979 by two researchers Robert Raskin and Calvin S. Hall.

As noted previously, narcissism is an excessive preoccupation with oneself, believing that one is superior to others. Narcissists have a grandiose perception of themselves, even though this is usually a façade. Men are also more likely to be narcissists than women. It is quite easy to consider someone confident in themselves or invested in their career a narcissist. Still, this trait runs much deeper than that. A lot of people perceive narcissists as overly confident people. But in truth, narcissists are far from it. Everything you think you know about the narcissist in your life is probably a smokescreen that may never be uncovered because of how smartly they cover the fragments of poor self-esteem that threaten to break through their façade. Unlike what you have in mind, being a narcissist does not automatically mean that you have a surplus of self-esteem and security. Narcissists have an excessive need for attention, admiration, and praise from others, and this need can only stem from low self-esteem levels. They also have a compulsive desire to be the center of attention, expect preferential treatment—reflecting a seemingly higher status—and are known for their lack of empathy for others' needs.

To some extent, it is okay to have some level of narcissism; however, when narcissism becomes out of control, it damages your personal, familial, and professional relationships.

Narcissists exhibit several characteristics that can be used to identify their personality. The following are some common ones.

The first thing to look out for in a person is their excessive need for admiration. A narcissistic partner or coworker loves to talk about themselves, and the only thing they expect from you is your attentiveness. If your partner likes to reel off about how their day at work went without ever asking of yours, that partner is more than likely a narcissist. They may never request to know things about you, and even if you manage to chip in something about yourself, they are always quick to divert the attention back to themselves. This behavior may make you feel annoyed, bored, or even drained, but these feelings never last. Many narcissists can beguile their audience (victim). They are usually charming, successful, talented, and beautiful, so much so that you are willing to let go of whatever feeling of annoyance you have about their behavior. You will be too enchanted to care about what they are doing to you. Keep in mind that narcissists are also very good at seduction. So, even when they act interested in you, it will wane over time. Narcissists make use of flattery a lot, especially when they are trying to win you over.

Not only do narcissists seek desperately for attention, but they also have a grandiose sense of self. They believe that they are special. They brag about their achievements in the bid to impress you. When you first meet one, you may not instantly pick up the level of their exaggerations unless you are already familiar with narcissism. If they are not yet accomplished, they may fantasize or brag about how they deserve more recognition than they get. All of these are borne of their need for constant validation, praise, and recognition from others. Since most narcissists tend to associate themselves with people of perceived high status, they may tell you about the celebrities they "claim to" know. They may wear the latest designer clothes, buy the latest expensive gadgets, or eat in the best restaurants. All this may entrance you, but they are symptoms of the narcissist's need to keep up a bedazzling façade to hide the emptiness they feel.

Narcissists are commonly known for their lack of empathy. Although people who are not narcissists may also be known for it, the lack of empathy is a vital and determining factor when added to their sense of entitlement and the inclination to exploit others. Always pay attention to their expressions when you tell a sad story and check out how they receive and react to the narration. Are they devoid of empathy for the tales of hardships and particularly insensitive to your needs? Tell a narcissist that you cannot do something that you promised to do for them— because of an injury or the loss of a loved one—and they will find a way to make it about how your disappointment will affect *them*. Some of the ways that a narcissist in your life may show their apparent lack of empathy include giving rude replies, ordering you around, not listening when you talk, ignoring boundaries, taking calls without permission when you are talking to them, etc. These little gestures may seem trivial or insignificant—since they don't actually hurt you—but they give an insight into the kind of person you are dealing with: someone who does not care about your feelings. If they act like that on minor issues, they will behave worse on issues that matter. Narcissists have a problem with vulnerability—whether it is theirs or yours. They are also unemotionally unavailable. Most narcissists will keep their distance once they see that you are getting closer to them. They do this because they don't want you to see the person that they really are behind the mask.

A psychological sense of entitlement is another common characteristic of narcissists. Their sense of entitlement explains why they believe that the world should revolve around them. Not only do they feel like they are superior to others, but they also expect to be treated specially. Narcissists do not adhere to rules, because they believe that these rules don't apply to them. A narcissist is never wrong—if anything is wrong, it is the rule of law. A narcissistic person expects you to accommodate their needs, no matter how inconvenient it makes you. Being in a relationship with someone narcissistic is one-sided, where you are the giver, and they are the receiver. If you are codependent, you are more likely to end up in a relationship with a narcissist. Codependent, in the most straightforward language, are people-pleasers, and narcissists and other dark personalities love people-pleasers.

Now, if there is one thing that is immediately evident in most narcissists, especially to psychology professionals, it is their willingness to exploit others for personal gain. As a normal person, this may be difficult to spot until you know the person better, but there are many ways you can tell. Basically, narcissists put themselves above every other person, which is how the D-factor manifests in this dark trait. However, it is difficult to immediately notice this because narcissists are also great at maintaining that façade and pretentious personality. Narcissistic individuals see others as objects to be used to serve their personal needs and wants. Once you start to feel used in your relationship, it means that your partner is exploiting you. However, exploitation doesn't only take place in romantic relationships. At work, a narcissistic colleague might take all the credit for something you both worked on. If you are a woman, you may feel like your partner is only using you to satisfy their sexual needs. This becomes apparent when the only time they care for you or your needs is when they want you in their bed. If you are a man, you may feel like your partner is using you for money. It can go both ways. Narcissists are masters of manipulation. They will influence you to do their bidding and make you feel like it is something you really want to do. Whether it is a personal, familial, or professional relationship, narcissists care nothing about your needs, feelings, wants, or person.

Because narcissists do not respect boundaries, they find it easy to exploit their victims.

Usually, it is easy to identify a narcissist when you know what to look out for—but some narcissists are harder to identify. These ones are *covert narcissists*. They have all the traits discussed above, yet you cannot easily identify them because they don't make it as obvious as the overt narcissist. In psychology, human behavior can be said to be overt or covert. Overt behaviors are those that you can easily observe and pick up in others, such as the narcissistic traits explained above. Covert behaviors, on the other hand, are subtle and much harder to pick up on.

Covert narcissists want admiration and praise as much as their overt counterparts. They also lack empathy. Yet, they do not seem to act like it. However, the truth is that they act on it, usually in ways that most people would not pick up on immediately. You are probably finding it hard to picture a narcissist that is subtle and covert in their approach. Picture this: You have your favorite song, and you are blasting it at the highest volume, compared to playing that same song on the lowest volume. In this example, the song is the same, but the volume at which you are playing it is different. This is the exact case with overt and covert narcissists. It is the same person, but with a different style and approach that is harder to observe.

The key difference between overt and covert narcissists is that covert narcissists are usually more introverted. You can easily identify an overt narcissist in the room because they tend to be arrogant, loud, and attention-thirsty. These behaviors are easily observable by anybody in the room. From the word "covert," you can easily assume that this means that the narcissist is sneaky, or their behavior is less exaggerated than a covert narcissist. But this is far from the truth; they have the same traits as an overt narcissist. Unlike overt narcissists, who would usually exaggerate their self-importance themselves, a covert narcissist may diminish their accomplishments to get reassurance from the people around them. They use more passive tactics to get attention and admiration from others. Rather than feed their need for self-importance, covert narcissists go around seeking reassurance about their skills, talents, and accomplishments.

Narcissists also like to shame and blame others for retaining that sense of being better than others. The overt narcissist does this by being blatantly rude, putting others down, criticizing maliciously, and acting sarcastically. On the other hand, the covert narcissist makes this less obvious. Rather than act loudly for all to see, they may gently approach you to explain why the blame is on you and not them. They play the victim and make it seem like *your* behavior has done something greatly hurtful to them. In fact, they may even take it a step further by emotionally abusing you so that you can reassure and praise them and ask for their forgiveness. The end goal of that "gentle" interaction is to make you feel small compared to them.

While covert narcissists are not necessarily sneaky, they sure love to confuse when they interact with others. Rather than blame and shame in some cases, they resort to causing you to question your belief of an event and second-guess yourself. This is just another way they create leverage between themselves and another person. The point of using tactics like this is to be at the top of the power pyramid in their relationships. Once they can get you to question and second-guess yourself, they have leeway to manipulate and exploit you even more. Due to their need to feel more important than others, covert narcissists will do anything to keep the spotlight on themselves. So, in a situation where an overt narcissist will discard you or manipulate you to achieve their goal, a covert narcissist will blatantly disregard you. Covert narcissists are grandmasters of not acknowledging a person when they choose. This is why narcissists tend to gravitate toward caring and compassionate individuals, such as codependents, empaths, etc. They recognize that people like this are easier to manipulate and exploit. However, the covert narcissist does it in a less obvious way. Rather than tell you straight up that you are of no value to them—as an overt narcissist would—they might leave your texts as "unread" or wait until the very last minute before they reply. They might also stand you up on a date, show up late for an event you invite them to, or never confirm the plans you make together. They have no regard for your time or interests. All of these are the tactics they use to make you feel neglected, unimportant, and irrelevant.

It is quite easy to get into a relationship with a narcissist—whether overt or covert—if your parents are narcissistic. When raised by a narcissistic parent, you tend to let narcissists feel familiar without realizing it. Plus, once you get into a relationship with a narcissist, it is not as easy to get out. Being in a relationship with a narcissist can be quite distressing. Not only will the relationship be emotionally exhausting and frightening, but it may also be financially draining, depending on what the narcissist wants from you. In the quest to boost their self-esteem, you may end up letting them damage your perception of yourself. Letting a narcissist know how you feel about their actions and behaviors is mostly fruitless too.

The best way to navigate a relationship—personal or professional—with a narcissist is to establish healthy boundaries that they cannot cross unless you allow them. It also helps to distance yourself from them emotionally. Understand that you may not control how you feel about a narcissistic partner, but you *do* have control over how you respond to them. Eventually, completely cutting ties may be the best way to handle your relationship with a narcissistic parent, partner, boss, or family member. Unless the narcissist accepts that there is a problem and is willing to take steps to solve the problem, cutting ties is the best way to handle your relationship with them. Otherwise, they may leave you emotionally distraught with shattered self-esteem.

To avoid getting entangled with a narcissist, reflect on the traits that have been discussed thus far, and find ways to prevent yourself from getting into similar scenarios.

Chapter Four: Psychopathy

The term "Psychopathy" was coined from two Greek words, *psykhe* and *pathos*. Together, these two words mean "sick mind" or "suffering soul." Considering that the term was coined around the late 1800s, you can see that humanity has long recognized the twistedness of psychopathy. Yet, psychopathy is often romanticized in the media. The media tends to portray it as a condition that afflicts charming and good-looking cold-blooded serial killers and their likes. But an individual does not have to be a serial killer to be psychopathic. In the late 1800s, psychopathy was thought of as a form of moral insanity. However, this perception started to change around the twentieth century when Hervey Cleckley, a psychiatrist, published his book, *The Mask of Insanity*, which detailed the traits and characters of psychopaths. These were psychopaths he was treating at Georgia's University Hospital. Cleckley referred to psychopaths as the "forgotten men of psychiatry."

In his book, Cleckley argued that many of the psychopaths were violent criminals. Yet, they were only kept in prison for a stint or released from the hospitals because they were diagnosed to be sane. He believed that this was because they could display "a perfect mask of genuine sanity." What this means is that Cleckley recognized psychopaths' ability to pull off normalcy. You could be in a relationship with a psychopath without realizing it. There would be no apparent signs because you don't even know there is something wrong with the person you are with. Unfortunately, the rally calls in Cleckley's book were generally ignored by the medical community. By the 1960s, the medical community, through the Diagnostic and Statistical Manual (DSM), had replaced psychopathy with "antisocial personality disorder." But it was noted that ASPD doesn't include some of the hallmark traits of psychopathic disorder, such as callousness and the absence of empathy. Although this classification by the DSM is still strongly accepted today, it is crucial to note that while psychopaths are generally antisocial, not everyone with ASPD is a psychopath.

As a dark personality trait, psychopathy is marked by a chilling lack of empathy and desensitization to other affective, emotional states. The ability to detach themselves from other people's experiences, coupled with the lack of empathy, is the main reason why psychopaths can effectively manipulate people to do what they want. As manipulative as psychopaths are, though, it is incredibly difficult to spot a psychopathic person. Similar to narcissists, psychopaths can be very charming. They seem normal. However, beneath that façade is the absence of anything remotely related to conscience. Psychopaths are antisocial, which is why psychopathy is usually misconstrued for antisocial personality disorder (ASPD)—otherwise referred to as sociopathy. Due to their antisocial nature, psychopaths more often than not gravitate toward criminal acts.

It can be incredibly challenging to treat psychopathy in adults, but some treatments exist to manage psychopathic behaviors in youth. Once psychopathy matures to the adult stage, individuals become resistant to any form of psychological treatment. Psychopaths can commit the most heinous acts while maintaining the charming demeanor that is hard to see beneath. Several factors, such as genetics, brain anatomy, and environment, may contribute to the development of psychopathy in an individual. However, researchers are not entirely sure about the specific cause of this dark trait. Like the other two traits in the dark triad, psychopathy occurs in a spectrum. This means that it exists from mild to extreme. Psychologists diagnose psychopathy using the Hare Psychopathy Checklist, which evaluates traits like the absence of empathy, impulsivity, and pathological lying, all of which are measured on a three-point scale. Each trait is checked based on whether it does not apply, applies to a specific extent, or fully applies to an individual.

The checklist that is used to assess whether a person is a psychopathic include:

- Superficial charm
- Pathological lying
- Manipulative behavior
- An exaggerated sense of self-worth
- Inclination to boredom
- A constant need for stimulation
- Lack of guilt, remorse
- Reduced affect (i.e., emotional responses)
- Lack of empathy
- Callousness
- Impulsivity and irresponsibility
- Parasitic behaviors
- Lack of behavioral controls
- Promiscuous behavior
- A tendency to avoid responsibility for individual actions
- Behavioral problems
- Short-term relationships
- Juvenile delinquency
- Criminal versatility

These are all the traits that psychologists check for when assessing a person for the psychopathic disorder. To ascertain whether you are dealing with a psychopath, you can also look out for them.

People with antisocial personality disorder are acknowledged as having a combination of traits that vary in severity and nature. Therefore, it is somewhat complicated to describe them with specific terminology. Many people use "psychopath" and "sociopath" interchangeably, apparently because people with both conditions blatantly tend to disregard rules and regulations. The difference, though, is those antisocial tendencies are often caused by a mix of social and environmental factors. In contrast, psychopathy is regarded as an innate trait. It appears to come from within. Nevertheless, different genetic and nongenetic factors play a part in developing antisocial traits, some of which are present in most psychopaths. Therefore, even though antisocial personality disorder overlaps with psychopathic disorder, they are two different conditions.

There are both male and female psychopaths. Psychopathy is not gender-exclusive; however, the trait is more prevalent in men than women. Also, female psychopaths tend to be distinct. As an example, studies suggest that female psychopaths are less inclined to physical violence than males. Additionally, they tend to experience anxiety more and have worse self-perception.

Due to the media, many people subconsciously associate psychopathy with violent and criminal behaviors. Once you hear the word "psychopath," your brain will most likely conjure the image of a notorious serial killer, like Ted Bundy. But the fact is that psychopathy is much more complicated than being a serial killer or violent criminal. Researchers have, of course, found a statistical connection between psychopathy scores and violence, as well as other criminal behaviors. The tendency to shift blame, irresponsibility, impulsivity and other antisocial characteristics suggest that psychopaths are more likely to exceed moral boundaries and do morally inconceivable things, such as threaten, hurt, or even kill another person. Yet the connection between psychopathy and violence isn't a linear one. Not all psychopaths are criminals or killers, even though they gravitate toward violence more than a normal person. Note that other pathological traits may contribute to aggressive or violent behaviors aside from psychopathy. An example is sadism, which will soon be detailed.

Thanks to the media portrayals of psychopaths as insatiable killers that do not stop until they are caught, most people don't believe that they can be around a psychopath without realizing it. "He doesn't look like he could hurt a whole human, so he can't be a psychopath." Well, as you can see, the media is wrong. A person doesn't have to murder to be a psychopath; in fact, there are probably less psychopathic killers than you know. The bad thing about the media's portrayal of psychopaths is that it makes them much harder to single out in a crowd. Unless you catch them wearing a black trench coat and walking down the alley at night with a crazy-induced look, you probably won't believe that someone you know is a possible psychopath.

Research shows that only one percent of the population has the traits required to be diagnosed as a psychopath. In hindsight, this might seem like a trivial stat, but when you look at it clearly, the reality dawns: one in every 100 individuals is a psychopath. And if you happen to know a lot of people, that means that your neighbor, friend, coworker, boss, or favorite social media influencer could be a psychopath. Perhaps the person sitting next to you at work or on the bus is a psychopath. To worsen things, this percentage doubles or even quadruples if you are someone in a high-powered position. The chances that you have a psychopath lurking around waiting to take advantage of you is huge. So, with this number of psychopaths possibly lurking around, how can you identify one? The more accustomed you are with psychopathic traits, the less likely you will fall victim to their superficial charms.

The first trait to look out for is manipulation. Psychopaths are incredibly manipulative. Think about the psychopaths you have watched on TV shows or read about in books—what is the common depiction of them? Manipulative behavior is one of the common depictions. While an average person may wonder how such malevolent characters can persuade anybody, the reality is that psychopaths are extraordinarily good at manipulation. Even though Ted Bundy was a heinous individual, he had a girlfriend who believed him to be the sweetest and most charming man ever to exist. And when this girlfriend became aware of who he was, he had another one who believed in his innocence until the end. In fact, she even got pregnant by him while he was on death row. Why would a woman or person generally believe in a serial killer even with the avalanche of evidence to show that they did what they were accused of doing? Manipulation and brainwashing. This shows just how manipulative psychopathic people can be.

Psychopaths are masters of reading people. They know how to size you up to look for an opening, a weakness to exploit. Even if you are just meeting them for the first time, they are ever ready to exploit any sign of vulnerability that you show to them. Interestingly, not everyone can quickly read others almost accurately, but most, if not all, psychopaths do. As a result of this ability, they find it easy to capitalize on another person's good heart. If you are dating a psychopath, don't be surprised to find out that they know things about you that you didn't even tell them. Psychopaths love to gather all kinds of information about people, just to use it to manipulate or exploit them in the future. If you know someone who is always pushing you to tell them personal things about yourself while volunteering very little about themselves, this person may be a psychopath.

There is nobody more charming than a psychopath, not even a narcissist. They are charming to a fault, but you will never recognize that fault. Although this is not to imply that every charming person you meet is a psychopath, the point is that every psychopath you meet will sweep you away with their charms on the first meeting. However, beneath the charm, they actually feel nothing for you. This is why superficial charms are one of the hallmark traits of a psychopath.

Since they can easily read you and gain access to the information you ordinarily would not share with people, psychopaths will hurt you without you even realizing that they could or would. Knowing your weaknesses and vulnerabilities, they have enough ammunition to use against you whenever they feel like you are no longer of worth to them. Often, a person will express disbelief and dismay when they find out that someone they wholeheartedly trusted and loved is a psychopathic personality. This is because they usually never see it coming. Psychopaths are harder to spot than narcissists.

Because they aim to use you, psychopaths always tell their victims what they want to hear. When you have been in a close relationship with a psychopath for a while, and eventually find out who they really are, you will find that they have been using you all along. In intimate interactions and relationships, psychopaths have perfected the art of telling their partner exactly what they want to hear. They often leave their unsuspecting partners wondering, "How do you always seem to know what I want?" Since they are incredibly charming, you are unlikely to know about their real intentions. Many family members and loved ones of psychopathic criminals often claim that they never noticed any sign of evil or cruelty—as seemingly difficult as that is to believe.

Humans are born with a conscience, but not psychopaths. Or maybe they simply lose their conscience as they mature into adults. Still, psychopaths are generally known to have no morality. You can only feel emotions such as guilt, remorse, shame, or empathy when your conscience is intact. As a result, psychopaths can easily commit unconscionable acts. In their head, a psychopath plays out different scenarios and plot where they commit their heinous acts with a fervor that you—as a normal human being—cannot even begin to comprehend or relate with. That said, psychopaths are not emotionally unresponsive to what they do to other people due to their lack of conscience.

To tell if someone you know is a potential psychopath, pay attention to the tone of their voice. Have you ever been able to rile them up to the point where they raise their voice? Probably not. Most psychopaths speak monotonously, so much so that you cannot detect the emotion they feel when they speak. In verbal delivery, there is a rise and fall of tone inflection when most people speak. This is a sign of the presence of emotions. It explains how voices may sound differently, depending on the emotions someone feels at a particular point. Psychopaths can't feel actual emotions, so this rise and fall of inflection are rarely apparent in their tone. It is easy to think that someone who has never lost their cool has mastered the art of controlling their emotions—when, in reality, they probably have psychopathic tendencies.

In psychology, empathy is associated with positivity. However, psychopathy is a dark trait; hence, psychopaths can't feel empathy. The lack of empathy is one of the prominent traits that can be used to identify a psychopath. Psychopaths cannot even feel their own pain, let alone someone else's. They are numb and don't care. Emotional detachment, minimal anxiety, and extreme narcissistic psychopathology are some of the characteristics displayed by psychopaths, as identified by J. Reid Maloy in the publication, *The Mark of Cain: Psychoanalytic Insight and the Psychopath.* Yet psychopaths respond to emotions such as anger and fear because these are feelings that they can readily exploit without feeling bad. Rather than feel bad, they gain a certain pleasure from exploiting these "weak" emotions. Interestingly, psychopaths themselves are resistant to feelings of fear—not that they are incapable of experiencing fear, but they find it difficult to detect and respond to fear in the way that normal humans would.

Other traits to watch out for include:

- A feeling of arrogance, superiority, and entitlement.
- A flagrant disregard for rules and order.
- Inconsistent work history.
- A string of marital breakups.
- A mastery of the art of lying and deception.

These are some of the traits that you can watch out for in a person to tell if they are psychopathic. If someone in your life seems to exhibit a combination of these traits, even in the littlest way possible, it is best to start taking steps to separate yourself from them. As much as many people would love to believe otherwise, you cannot manage a psychopath or cause them to change. However, keep in mind that displaying one or two of the traits discussed above does not automatically make a person a psychopath.

Chapter Five: Machiavellianism

Machiavellians are the ultimate masters of manipulation. The thing about Machiavellians is that they do not even have to learn manipulation; it just comes naturally to them. In fact, some of them probably don't even want to be manipulators. Those who have natural manipulation are High Machs. As a personality type, Machiavellianism is when a person focuses on self-interest, so much so that they will lie, deceive, manipulate, and exploit others to accomplish a goal. The term "Machiavellianism" is derived from the name of Niccolò Machiavelli, a philosopher who is renowned for the title, *The Prince*. In his book, Machiavelli espoused his views on how rulers should take a strict and harsh leadership approach. He believed that as long as glory and survival are the end goal, any means should apply to the ruling, regardless of whether the means are immoral, brutal, and inhumane. According to Machiavelli, virtues such as honesty, loyalty, etc., are expendable if vices like deceit will help you achieve your goals. To put it succinctly, he believed that leaders should adopt a Machiavellian style of ruling even if it is not something they are naturally inclined to use.

Machiavellianism became a very popular term in the late sixteenth century and was mainly used to describe the act of using deception to get ahead in life. It wasn't until the 1970s that it became recognized as a psychological term. Social psychologists Richard Christie and Florence L. Geis developed what was known as the "Machiavellianism Scale" or "Mach-IV Test." This is a personality inventory used for assessing Machiavellianism in people. Although research shows that Machiavellianism is more commonly found in men, anyone can be a Machiavellian, including children.

Although some people read *The Prince* and other Machiavellianism-themed books to learn the art of deception, real Machiavellians have a natural knack for deception and duplicity. They are intuitively inclined to be conniving, calculating, and deceptive. Basically, they will use you as a stepping stone to achieving their goals if you appear to be of use. Machiavellians are essentially amoral. They generally have the mindset that people who allow themselves to be used deserve it. In other words, if you get duped by a con artist, it is because you are stupid, and you deserve it—the con artist isn't to blame.

Humans are innately predisposed to be duplicitous, depending on the needs or situation they find themselves in. If you have ever lied about being sick just to avoid going to work or intentionally skip some details while narrating to your partner about how you met an ex recently, it means that you have the natural human capacity to dupe or con others to satisfy your own interest(s). Episodes like this rarely reflect the standard behavioral pattern for many people, and most feel guilty when they lie or take advantage of others. However, for Machiavellians, this is normal behavior. In fact, they don't behave any other way. It is a routine, and they stick to it fervently. Even if you catch a Machiavellian lying about something, they would rather find their way around it than admit to lying.

How does the D-factor manifest in Machiavellians? It is straightforward—they would step on literally anybody to achieve their goals. They are known to focus on their interests alone. Machiavellians prioritize themselves over any other person; thus, they can cause you harm if it means that they will meet their needs or achieve a goal. Like narcissists and psychopaths, Machiavellians are charming and confident. Winning people over is like reading the ABCs to them. They can readily win you over with flattery, and you won't even realize that you are being lied to or manipulated. Machiavellians lack morals, principles, and values. Although they don't completely lack empathy—like psychopaths—they certainly have impaired empathy levels, which is why they can deceive others without feeling regret.

The Machiavellianism scale is measured on a scale of up to 100. If a person scores above 60 on the test, they are regarded as High Machs, while people who score below 60 are called Low Machs. High Machs focus on self-interest and personal wellbeing more than anything. They believe that one must master the art of deception if one is to get ahead in life. High Machs do not believe that people can be innately good, so they are highly skeptical of human goodness. They also believe that trusting people is naïve. Because they prioritize power and success over any other thing, including love and relationships, they don't care about kindness or goodness. Low Machs, on the other hand, are more empathetic than High Machs. They display higher levels of empathy and are trusting and honest—to an extent. They also believe that humans are inherently good and that sticking to good morals can help one get ahead in life. However, if they fall too low on the Machiavellian Scale, they become too submissive and agreeable.

Though Machiavellianism is a separate trait from the other two traits in the dark triad, one person can sometimes have a combination of the three deadly traits. If an individual has all three dark traits, they can be potentially dangerous to the people around them. Yet, despite the evident connection between the dark triad traits and the prominence of one trait occurring with the other two in many people, there has to be concrete evidence that proves a correlation between the three traits. People with Narcissistic Personality Disorder (NPD) and Antisocial Personality Disorder (ASPD) tend to have certain Machiavellian traits. Research also found that Machiavellians tend to have high levels of depression, making them prone to depressive disorders.

How do you identify a Machiavellian? Firstly, they have a cold and calculating perception of you—even if they don't show it. Machiavellians are highly strategic; they will lie, cheat, and deceive if that is required to get what they want from you. Due to their inherent ability to emotionally detach, there is very little holding a Machiavellian back from taking advantage of or even harming you to get what they need. This is one of the reasons why Machiavellian views are considered problematic and aversive. If you know anyone who subscribes to the political philosophy of Niccolò Machiavelli, you are better off without them in your life. Similarly to psychopaths, Machiavellians will always put their personal needs and advancement before any other person.

In psychology, empathy is regarded from two points of view: cognitive and emotional. Cognitive empathy is referred to as being "cold," and emotional empathy is "hot." To be specific, cognitive or cold empathy is your understanding of how someone may be thinking, how they are likely to act in a situation, and how they are likely to interpret certain events. For example, a team manager may use cognitive empathy to understand the series of actions that may be triggered when they provide negative feedback about a project to their team: some of which could involve disagreement, defensiveness, and eventually, acceptance of the feedback. In the same case, the manager may use emotional empathy to resonate with their team. They may think, "My team will be extremely disappointed when I give them this feedback, so I have to be as constructive as possible." In the latter scenario, emotional empathy will help the manager shape their use of words in the feedback to lessen the impact on their team. This is to avoid emotionally hurting their team.

In comparison, a Machiavellian manager may cognitively empathize with his or her team, but find emotional empathy impossible. Simply put, they know what the team will think when they give them the feedback but cannot resonate with how they would react to the news emotionally. As a result, they will be unable to give the message in the most constructive way possible, thus coming across as harsh and insensitive—without realizing the emotional hurt caused to the team. Now, here is the interesting thing: Machiavellians need cognitive empathy to exploit others. Deceptions and manipulation require you to understand the cognitive process of your victim. Machiavellians know the reaction to expect when they tell you a particular thing, and what to expect if they say another thing. That ability to cognitively empathize with you is what they use to their advantage when they lie, deceive, and exploit your kindness, weaknesses, and vulnerability.

Even more interesting, research has shown that some High Machs can emotionally empathize with others; yet, they simply don't care about how their actions hurt you. Specifically, researchers discovered that some Machiavellians subset can "bypass empathy." That is, they have the full human capacity to understand the thoughts and feelings that may arise as a result of being deceived, manipulated, or lied to, but they go ahead with their malicious intent. This apparent lack of moral conscience has been considered an evolutionary advantage by many psychology researchers. This implies that Machiavellians have the advantage of pursuing their goals unabashedly without being held back by moral considerations. If a Machiavellian sets their eyes on something, they get it no matter what. However, there is a rising question in the scientific community about the possibility of Machiavellians forming long-lasting, mutually-satisfying relationships with other people if they can't even resonate with others emotionally, or care for their thoughts and feelings.

Machiavellians have a reduced theory of mind—the ability to understand why people think in individually unique ways. Although similar, theory of mind is different from cognitive empathy because it covers a broader range from goals to aspirations, desires, and information in a person's head. Whereas cognitive empathy is just about the changes in thinking and feeling from moment to moment. To manipulate others, Machiavellians need to have a significant understanding of the drive behind their victims' actions and behaviors. However, research shows that Machiavellianism negatively links with the theory of mind and social-cooperative skills. This suggests that even though they appear to be, Machiavellians may not be as great at understanding and manipulating others as they think. Thus, while Machiavellianism comprises a set of beliefs and values about deceiving others to get what you want, there is no guarantee for Machiavellians that their deception and manipulation will be successful.

Psychologists believe that behavior is driven by two individual neurological systems that are separate from each other: the behavioral activation system and the behavioral inhibition system. This is based on Grey's reinforcement sensitivity theory. The behavioral activation system is linked with tendencies such as social behavior, extraversion, and action-taking. In comparison, the behavioral inhibition system is connected with tendencies such as withdrawn behavior, introversion, and thinking instead of taking action. This means that the behavioral activation system is about approach, while the behavioral inhibition system is about avoidance. According to the latest research on the dark triad, psychopathy and narcissism are linked to greater activity levels in the behavioral activation system.

In comparison, Machiavellianism is linked with higher levels of activity in the behavioral inhibition system. Therefore, narcissists and psychopaths are more likely to take action and socialize with others, so they engage in approach behaviors more. Machiavellians, on the other hand, are more likely to avoid socializing with others. They depend on their thoughts and intuition more, so they engage in avoidant and withdrawn behavior. This correlates with the description of Machiavellians as cold, calculating manipulators who are always looking for ways to plot and exploit others, rather than proactively violating their humanity as psychopaths would.

Machiavellianism is linked with alexithymia, which is the inability to recognize, label, and understand one's emotions properly. Alexithymic people tend to be cold, aloof, and detached from their emotional experiences. In Machiavellians, alexithymia may result from an inability to understand emotions, due to the shallow experience of emotions, or a decreased theory of mind and empathetic ability. Regardless of whatever the cause is, studies show that Machiavellians are very cognitive—more than emotional—in how they approach others and themselves. They are also normally out of tune with their emotional states. So, if a Machiavellian felt guilty for conning an innocent lady, they wouldn't even realize it.

The conclusion is that Machiavellianism involves having a cold and calculating perception of the world and its people. This perception makes it easier to take advantage of other people because you believe they would do it to you first if they had the chance. Both cognitively and emotionally, Machiavellians cannot properly resonate with others.

As evident from all three dark traits, one prevalent thing is the inclination to put yourself before everything. They are all about self-interest—putting yourself first to achieve what you want regardless of how that affects other people. However, narcissism, psychopathy, and Machiavellianism all have a different objective or focus.

For narcissism, the focus is that you are superior to every other person, and you deserve to get admiration and be treated better than others. Narcissists believe that they should be treated differently from the rest of the world.

Machiavellianism is mostly about manipulating and deceiving others for personal advancement. No more, no less. In a way, Machiavellians also believe that they are better than others, but not in the same sense as narcissists.

Psychopathy is completely about the lack of empathy, remorse, or guilt, which means that psychopaths can do anything to anybody without feeling remotely bad about their actions.

Chapter Six: Sadism

Usually, a human being would try to avoid making others feel pain or suffer. Even when you do something to hurt another person, you feel guilt or another feeling of distress. But there are some people for whom cruelty is pleasurable. Hurting other people gives them a sense of excitement and pleasure that nothing else can offer, and according to new research, people like this are quite common. These people are referred to as sadists, and their personality trait is sadism. Thus, some scientific community members believe that sadism should be included in the dark triad—and for good reasons.

Like many people, you might have been exposed to your first depiction of sadism in the *Fifty Shades of Grey* novels and films. The series brought a depiction of what sadism looks like in the bedroom. Still, it failed to really let people understand that sadism can be much worse. As a result of the series, many people now have a warped and romanticized view of narcissism. Suddenly, everyone wants a "Christin Grey" type of guy. However, what people do not know is that sadism can be much more pervasive and mundane than its portrayal in the *Fifty Shades of Grey* trilogy.

Deep within the recesses of many people's minds is a different type of sadism altogether—one that doesn't care about love or anything like it. People with dark triad traits are callous individuals who view other people as tools to exploit for their advantage. Taking pleasure in others' suffering is the hallmark trait of sadism and regarded as an aspect of the frame in the constellation of the dark triad traits.

But personality psychologists are starting to believe that a penchant for cruelty is separate in understanding why an individual wants to harm another person. Simply put, it stands on its own. However, rather than being exhibited in ways that would have negative consequences, such as humiliation or even death, everyday sadism is being expressed in benign and subtle ways. This means that even if you were to be living with a sadist, you wouldn't realize it. You also might be expressing the benign form of sadism without knowing it. You don't necessarily have to hurt someone around you. It may be that you get a certain thrill when you blast your opponents in *Mortal Kombat* or any other video games. When you are with friends, you may push for them to get into a violent fight that involves breaking bottles and hurting each other really badly. Your favorite genre may be action thrillers that involve battles where many lives are lost. Perhaps your favorite scene in the series *Merlin* is when the knights have to fight to the death. Maybe you still relive the scenes in your head. Common in all of these scenarios is that you are gaining pleasure from normal experiences in which cruelty is indirectly experienced.

In September 2013, a study named *The Behavioral Confirmation of Everyday Sadism* was conducted to determine if everyday sadists had a predilection to inflict real, not just imagined, harm to others. The researchers believed that these overt sadists were likely to become more aggressive than normal human beings when provoked. Furthermore, they suggested that sadism is likely to give a unique proclivity for antisocial behaviors above and beyond the traits normally associated with the dark triad personalities. In other words, sadists tend to be much more malicious than narcissists, psychopaths, and Machiavellians.

To find out how overt sadism manifests in everyday behaviors, researchers conducted a laboratory task that involved mimicking the type of cursory harm-inducing behavior that people might, knowingly or unknowingly, perform daily. The researchers decided to use bug killing as the test to identify possible sadism in seemingly regular people. According to the lead researcher, the willingness to kill a bug would establish a sadistic desire to inflict harm via direct physical contact. To test this theory, the participants were offered a choice to perform certain unpleasant tasks, with the option of killing bugs, as well as other unpleasant but non-sadistic options. They agreed on three options (including bug killing) as tasks that a participant could choose: helping somebody else kill bugs, putting their hand in a barrel of ice water, and cleaning dirty toilets. To fish out the overt sadists among the participants, the team used the Short Sadistic Impulse Scale—developed in 2011 by a team of psychologists from the University of College Cork. The team also included questionnaires on dark triad traits to distinguish the qualities of sadism from narcissism, psychopathy, and Machiavellianism. Expectedly, individuals with high levels of sadism chose to kill the bugs than over the other options. After concluding the task, they also reported that they enjoyed that specific task the most. Interestingly, those who had chosen an alternative task regretted not choosing the bug-killing task.

In the second part of the laboratory test, the highly sadistic individuals were rated in comparison with those that were less cruelty-inclined. They were willingly asked to participate in a button-pushing competition that involved attacking a participant that they feel would not attack them back. Throughout the test, the participants were given the privilege to explode white noise into their opponents' headset for each trial they won. Of course, there was no actual opponent. However, the participants were made to believe that they wouldn't be attacked back by their opponents after being ear-blasted.

The second aspect of the laboratory test was to answer if the highly sadistic individuals would willingly continue to attack and cause distress to a non-attacking opponent. The result was that those who were rated as being highly sadistic did not only take the opportunity to harm their supposed opponents, but they also worked extra hard for the chance to blast their opponents some more. It gave them a certain sort of thrill and satisfaction to know that they were hurting another person with no chance of being reprehended or attacked back. The dark triad traits, in the bug killing tasks, didn't accurately predict the outcome of the noise-blasting inclinations—but sadism did. Hence, there is good evidence to suggest that people who score high on a sadism measurement scale or questionnaire are inclined to behave in casual ways that are similar to the laboratory tasks.

It is hard to say *exactly* what the cause of sadism is; after all, what could make a human being derive so much pleasure from inflicting pain on a fellow human being? The very idea is difficult to grasp for the average person. Yet many people embrace this kind of lifestyle, willingly or otherwise. There is no known cause of sadism, unfortunately. However, different theories try to provide possible explanations for sadistic behaviors in certain people.

One explanation is that sadists have been harshly abused and violated— physically, emotionally, and sexually—in their childhood. The abuse is also not just a one-time thing—it had to be constant and perpetually pervasive. Unpleasant experiences in childhood or early adolescence are regarded as a major cause of a sadistic personality. It has also been discovered that sadism can be acquired through learning or observation. For example, constantly finding oneself in situations where sexual enjoyment is derived from others' anguish can result in the development of a sadistic personality or sadomasochistic behaviors. An individual does not even have to take part—it counts as sadism if observing the suffering makes a person feel good. If you have read the *Fifty Shades of Grey* book series, you know that Christian Grey, the sadistic character, didn't even exhibit traits of sadism until he was introduced to the sexual aspect of it by his mother's good friend—despite him being abused emotionally and physically as a child. So, it is safe to say that he developed a sadistic personality through learning and observation. Then, he became an active participant.

Here are the basic characteristics to help you identify a sadist based on questions from the Short Sadistic Impulse Scale (SSIS):

- They genuinely enjoy seeing people get hurt.
- Sadists fantasize about hurting people physically, emotionally, and sexually. Even if they have never acted on these fantasies, there is every possibility that they will one day.
- Sadists think the idea of hurting people or animals is exciting.
- They have likely hurt another person for their own enjoyment before.
- They believe that people generally would hurt another person if they had the opportunity. That is their operative mindset.
- They will hurt you if you are at their mercy.
- They humiliate others just to lord their superiority over them.
- They get physically violent when they are extremely angry.

Sadistic individuals not only display sadistic acts, but they also enjoy them. People who are highly sadistic exhibit recurring cruel and aggressive behavior. But sadism isn't always physical; it also includes emotionally manipulating others using fear, emotional cruelty, and obsession with violence. Parents who love to disciple their children using corporal punishment may or may not be sadists. As noted, sadism can be psychological. For example: Say someone knows that you have a fear of spiders. If this person constantly taunts you with that fear by fake-alerting you to a spider—under your bed, on your shirt, or any other place—knowing the distress it will cause, they might be a sadist. They may genuinely enjoy watching you suffer from fear. If they keep using this fear against you, it means that your distress gives them pleasure—a hallmark trait of sadism.

Another way sadism can be used psychologically, particularly in a relationship, is if a partner keeps using something they know about their partner to cause them distress. A High Mach may do this to get something they want from their partner. A narcissist will likely do it to make themselves feel better than them. A psychopath will do something like that without remorse. Comparatively, a sadist will do it just to watch you in distress—no other reason. They want to see you suffer emotionally.

In its most pervasive form, sadism can become sexual sadism disorder. Sexual sadism disorder is one of the many psychiatric sexual disorders grouped as paraphilic disorders. Paraphilias are sexual fantasies, preferences, urges, and behaviors outside the spectrum of what is considered normal. However, they are considered signs of a disorder only if they manifest in behaviors that are potentially harmful or distressing to oneself or others, particularly if they happen without consent. Sexual sadism manifests as a thrilling feeling that results from humiliating and inflicting pain on another person to achieve sexual gratification. In this case, the pain and humiliation may not be imagined; it is sometimes real. Moreover, it can be physical or psychological, depending on what the sadist likes. Actually, sadism is derived from the name of a French Aristocrat, Marquis de Sade, who was known for writing books around the theme of administering plain to gain sexual pleasure. This explains why sadism is mostly associated with sexual activities, even though it may be expressed in other ways.

Sadistic acts that may be potentially harmful to others include restraint (with chains, handcuffs, or ropes), spanking, beating, whipping, biting, or imprisonment. If a person can establish a mutually-satisfying sexual, sadistic relationship with a willing partner without causing them distress or dysfunction, they are not categorizable as having a sexual sadism disorder. But when they repeatedly engage in sadistic sexual acts without seeking their partner's consent, they may be diagnosed with sexual sadism disorder. They may also be diagnosed if the sadistic thoughts, fantasies, or behaviors result in social, professional, and other functional problems. Extreme sexual sadistic acts are potentially dangerous and could lead to death; hence, they can be regarded as criminal acts.

For a person to get diagnosed with sexual sadism disorder, they must have repeatedly and persistently fantasized or caused the physical or mental distress of another person—with or without consent—to achieve intense sexual arousal and gratification. These symptoms must also be monitored and observed for a minimum of six months before SSD can be diagnosed. Other traits such as impulsivity, dishonesty, and an absence of empathy and remorse may also be present before a diagnosis can occur.

Thanks to the popularity of *Fifty Shades of Grey* and other copycat movies that center around sadism, it appears that people are opening up more to learning about this personality type. Sadism is a part of the human experience, and sadly, people must accept that. Fortunately, only a minority of people are actually willing to act upon the innate human desire to inflict pain on others for pleasure. Nevertheless, the media must stop romanticizing the concept of sadism. People need to understand just how aversive sadism can get. Some people could make the mistake of getting into a relationship with a sadist—thinking it will be just as it is with their favorite characters in the books and movies. Unfortunately, reality often turns out to be completely different.

The problem with people with all four malevolent traits and sadism, as discussed thus far, is that individuals with these personalities are unlikely to want to change or seek therapy. While narcissists may still go to therapy and achieve treatment, the possibility is slimmer for psychopaths and Machiavellians. Even then, they may not go to therapy unless pushed by loved ones or because the court has ordered them to attend therapy after committing a crime. The chance of either option happening is almost nonexistent—especially because most family members do not even know anything is wrong. Even when they do see that something is wrong, they don't accept it unless the affected person is outright violent toward others.

The subsequent chapters look at some of the known and unknown techniques used by narcissists, psychopaths, Machiavellians, and sadists to manipulate and exploit their victims.

Chapter Seven: Gaslighters and Emotional Manipulation

Gaslighting is a form of emotional manipulation that can potentially turn a person insane if one is not careful. Unfortunately, it is also a very effective tool used by people with the dark triad traits to take advantage of their unsuspecting victims. More than ever, attention is being shone on the concept of gaslighting and gaslighters, which is a good thing. The term is everywhere, from clinical literature to social media. Even though people on social media may be using the term a tad wrongly, everyone gets the idea that gaslighting is a form of emotional manipulation, and gaslighters are emotional manipulators. The problem now is how one can identify when they are being gaslighted.

Gaslighting is inherently manipulative behavior. It is a very powerful form of emotional abuse, albeit more subtle than other techniques. Gaslighting involves driving a person to the point where they begin to question their sanity. Simply put, gaslighters seek to distort your perception of reality to the point where you can no longer believe in yourself. It is a mind game that abusers use to establish control over their victims. Like any type of abuse, gaslighting can be used in any relationship, including social, personal, and professional relationships. Gaslighters can be anybody from a social media celebrity to a public figure or even someone holding a position of power. They could be your sibling, parent, boss, coworker, boyfriend, girlfriend, close friend, or a close relative. Basically, you can be gaslighted by anybody you have around you, regardless of whatever position they hold in your life.

Gaslighting is commonly used by narcissists, abusive partners, and people such as cult leaders. The effect of the emotional abuse on a victim can be devastating.

How does psychology define gaslighting? In psychology, gaslighting is defined as a form of emotional and psychological abuse used to alter or entirely eradicate another individual's perception of reality to gain influence, control, and power over them. Gaslighters use subtle mind games and manipulation tactics, which are executed in phases until they achieve their aim. To undermine the sanity and stability of their victim, a gaslighter repeats the manipulation tactics regularly. Eventually, the victim starts to doubt their own judgment and perceptions of issues, memories, or versions of events that have happened. If the gaslighting is not stopped in time, the victim starts losing their sense of self and self-worth. In other words, they forget who they are and become whom their abuser tells them they are.

The term "gaslighting" originated from a play written in 1938 by Patrick Hamilton, a British playwright. Later, the play was adapted into a movie, *Gaslight* (1944), which is when the term became popular. The film depicts a young woman who married too early to a manipulative and controlling husband. In his attempts to keep her subjugated, the husband manipulated her surrounding in specific ways that made her question her perceptions of reality. In the film, they had gas lights in the home. To undermine his wife's sanity, the husband would dim the lights and cause them to flicker. When the wife questioned him about what was happening, he would deny that anything was happening. He would specifically call her "crazy" and tell her nothing was wrong with the gas lights. As a result, the wife started thinking that she was crazy. She was emotionally traumatized and almost lost her mind. Eventually, she would find someone who confirmed that the events were not just happening in her head. In the end, she left the marriage because she realized the kind of man her husband was.

Abuse takes a different form, but people are mostly conscious of physical and sexual abuse. Verbal and emotional abuse do not receive as much attention as the other two. Abuse can be physical, emotional, mental, verbal, sexual, and even financial. While other forms of abuse are easily identifiable, it is not as straightforward to detect when you are being gaslighted by someone you are close to. Gaslighting is done in different ways, usually stage by stage, until an individual completely loses control of their perception.

The first form of gaslighting takes is the "lie and denial" form. Gaslighters are liars, but they don't just lie once in a while—lying is a habit. Lies and denial are the biggest tools that gaslighters use to alter their victim's perception of events effectively. They establish their abusive pattern by telling lies, lies, and more lies. When a gaslighter lies to you, and you catch them lying, they don't accept it—they deny. Then you, as the victim, start to question yourself and become unsure about the simplest situations. Their goal is to put you in a state of constant self-doubt and confusion. Once you are, you have no choice but to go to them for clarity—which is exactly what they want. Unfortunately, seeking clarity from the gaslighter results in a cycle of abuse that leaves you feeling more uncertain and vulnerable day by day.

Example:

Romana catches her boyfriend, Mark, trying to get another girl's mobile number at the mall. Angry, she confronts him, but he blatantly denies doing this. Even when Romana tells him that she clearly saw him, he tells her that she must have been imagining things because he never tried to get any girl's number. Romana feels conflicted because she definitely saw him, but she decides to let it go since he denies it.

The second is the *projection*. Your gaslighter loves to project; in fact, it is their signature tool. Gaslighters have the worst behaviors—they lie, cheat, manipulate, and perpetuate negative thinking. Now, here is the problem: they start to project all of these behaviors onto you. Whatever bad behavior they get caught or don't get caught doing will be assigned to you. Every immoral characteristic they are known for will be projected onto you. In the bid to exonerate yourself from the things you are being accused of, you become distracted from the gaslighter— who is engaging in these behaviors. You will be too preoccupied with defending yourself to realize that you are being accused of things that the other person is doing. To make it worse, the gaslighter will repeatedly project these behaviors onto you to control the narrative and your relationship.

Example:

The next day, Mark reflects on the accusation and tells Romana that he believes the only reason she would accuse him of something like that was that she was cheating on him. He starts giving instances when he saw Romana talking to other guys—how the conversation didn't seem completely harmless—but he never accused Romana of anything. The following day, he repeats this. It becomes a habit as he casually implies that Romana talks to other guys whenever she's on her phone. Romana becomes regretful and starts wondering why she even thought the worst of Mark in the first place. She begins seeing herself as a bad person in the relationship.

Next, the gaslighter shows an apparent *lack of congruence* in their words and actions. You just do not find the congruence in what they say and how they act. The mismatch in speech and action is evident to the victim in the initial stage. A gaslighter will tell you one thing and do something else. They make promises and commitments without fulfilling them—deliberately. They weaponize kind and loving words to make you relax over a specific situation. What you should keep in kind is that the gaslighter isn't authentic, and neither are their words. Paying attention to how much the words match the actions will give you insight into whether you are dealing with a gaslighter.

Example:

After a while, Mark promises to stop accusing Romana of cheating. He says that he is tired of fighting. He promises Romana that he loves her and would never consider loving any other girl. Unfortunately, the next day, Roman catches him red-handed once again—he's talking to the same girl from the mall. Romana is conflicted about whether to confront him again. Eventually, she does. However, he tells her, "Baby, I thought we agreed to stop fighting. You realize how much I love you? Do you genuinely think I would ever hurt you like that? I can't even imagine hurting you in that way." Romana feels good hearing these things from him, but she has no idea how inauthentic they are.

Gaslighting is also done through *refusal and memory challenges.* A gaslighter will never accept or listen to their victim's concerns. They would rather pretend not to understand what you are saying. They try to make you feel stupid for talking to them to the point where you might even question your lucidity. They will also challenge your memory of events. They deny the details of an event as you remember it. Or, they will deny such a thing ever happened. This further makes you question your memory. A gaslighter may even take it up a notch and create falsified details of the event.

Example:

When Romana confronts Mark once again, he asks her what she is talking about. He claims that he doesn't remember talking to anybody on the phone. In fact, he tells her that the person he remembers talking to was his cousin, whom she knows well. When Romana tries to say that she heard the girl's name from the mall, he shuts her down and says he doesn't even remember the girl anymore. He says he wouldn't have even remembered her if Romana hadn't brought the girl up again. Romana feels bad and concludes that she must have imagined hearing the name since it's still on her mind. She apologizes to Mark.

Consequently, the gaslighter starts to isolate the partner from friends and loved ones. They know that you are already questioning your sanity, so they make this worse by isolating you from the rest of the world. This way, you have no choice but to go to them for clarity on the situation. They may even start to refer to you as a "crazy person." In doing this, they start to turn you against your family and friends, and vice versa. In most cases, your loved ones may not even know what the gaslighter is saying. Gaslighters try to make their victims believe that their family doesn't care about them. "Are you sure Katrina is really your best friend? Why doesn't she come around to see you more often?" Statements like this are used to isolate you from your loved ones so that the gaslighter can gain more control over your life.

Example:

Mark tells Romana that he doesn't think they should hang out with their friend anymore. After all, it is when they go out that misassumptions occur and result in fights. How would they fight over a mysterious girl if they don't even go out in the first place? Romana agrees with him because she is willing to do everything to make their relationship work out.

Eventually, Mark and Romana, in the examples above, form a codependent relationship. Codependency is defined as excessive emotional and psychological reliance on one's partner. In a relationship where one partner is constantly being gaslighted, the gaslighter incites feelings of anxiety and insecurity in the gaslightee—to gain control over them. After a while, the partner being gaslighted has no choice but to cede control over to the gaslighter. When this happens, the gaslighter becomes the dictator in the relationship. They have control over acceptance, security, safety, respect, and approval. They can choose to give or take them away. Codependent relationships are established on a foundation of vulnerability, fear, and marginalization.

Although gaslighting in itself is not a disorder, there are several reasons personality traits that make a person a gaslighter.

Gaslighters exhibit an authoritarian personality, which is found in narcissists, psychopaths, Machiavellians, and sadists. People with authoritarian personality types rarely find faults in themselves. Still, they are quick to point out the faults and shortcomings of other people. If someone is a gaslighter, they likely have a personality disorder fueling that behavior.

The ultimate goal of a gaslighter is to dominate, control, and exploit. But some gaslighters do not limit their victims to one person at a time. They are ambitious and may attempt to dominate and exploit a group of people, or a whole community of people. By creating a pattern of lies, denials, and coercions, the gaslighter can keep the gaslightees in a never-ending state of self-doubt, insecurity, and fear. This gives them the room to exploit them at will continuously, all for nothing more than personal advancement and power.

How do you identify a gaslighter in your life?

- They tell outright lies with a straight face. Even though you know they are lying, you become unsure because they tell this lie with such a straight face. They do this to establish a precedent to keep you unsure and unstable. You never know what to expect from them next.

- Even when you offer proof in their face, they deny something ever happened. You hear them say something, clearly, but they deny ever saying it when you ask them about it. This makes you start doubting what you know you heard—maybe it was something else, maybe they really never said it. The more denials occur, the more your reality becomes distorted. This leaves with you no choice but to accept their reality as yours.

- They manipulate you with the things that are dear to you the most. If you have kids, they may tell you that you'd be a better person if you never had them. If you know yourself to be an intelligent person, they may tell you that your intelligence doesn't matter alongside your negative traits. They target the very core of your person and use those things that are of the most value to you as ammunition.

- Over time, you start to feel worn out from the constant lies and denials. Since gaslighting is a gradual process, you may not quickly realize that you are wearing down. A lie there, plus a denial, a criticism regularly—it starts building up rapidly. Before you know it, you have been completely sucked into the web of manipulation. Even the most mindful person can get sucked into gaslighting without realizing it.

- They occasionally praise you and give positive criticism. This is a strategy to confuse you even more. Now, you have to wonder if the same person that said you weren't good enough the other day is also complimenting you? You start to think, "Oh, maybe they aren't so bad after all." But of course, they are. They are also calculating, and everything they do is to throw you off-balance, so you never know what to expect from them.

If you have someone in your life that you cannot predict even in the slightest sense of the word, this person is more than likely a gaslighter. Being in a relationship, intimate or otherwise, should be about normalcy and stability. This is not achievable with a gaslighter. They know that confusion disrupts and weakens people, so they continuously do things to uproot your feelings of stability. At the end of the day, you have no choice but to turn to them for the stability you want. One thing that is particularly interesting about gaslighters is that they will go to any length to convince you that someone else is a liar. By convincing you that someone you love is a liar, they are making you question your reality. After all, why would they call the person a liar if that weren't the case? Well, they can because they are a liar. Telling you other people are liars is a manipulation technique that makes you turn to them for the truth. They become the only one you have to turn to for correct information—which is really their "correct" information that is wrong.

The more familiar you are with the techniques used by gaslighters to gain control and dominance over their victims, the faster you will fish them out in a group of people so that you do not fall victim to their trap.

Chapter Eight: How to Detect a Lie through Body Language

Lying is part of human nature. Everyone has told at least one lie in their lifetime. Remember that time you lied to your friends to get out of a hangout that had been planned and agreed on eons ago? Some people lie to get out of situations they do not want to be in. Others lie to get in a situation they want to be in. The point is that people lie all the time. In fact, some people lie more than others. While some people lie with malicious intent, some tell lies to avoid hurting another person's feelings. For instance, if your best friend of many years suddenly confesses love for you, you may feel inclined to tell them that you share their feelings even if you don't. However, lying can be detrimental to your relationships, so it is best not to lie at all. Lies can vary in severity. Some are little white lies, some are serious, and some are sinister. Surprisingly, many people are bad at detecting when they are being lied to. After hundreds of studies on deception researchers found that the average person can only effectively detect lying 54 percent of the time. At first consideration, this may seem pretty impressive. But it becomes less impressive when you realize that 50 percent of the detection rate occurs by happenstance.

Plus, if people lie a lot, how do you know when you are being lied to by someone you know or possibly trust? Unless you are naturally psychic or have some magical power, there is no outright way to tell when you are being lied to. Obviously, it is difficult to measure and distinguish behavioral differences between liars and honest individuals. Research has been conducted to try to uncover different ways one can detect a lie. While there is no definitive sign to look out for, many helpful indicators of lying have been discovered by researchers. Fortunately, though, paying attention to body language while someone is talking may give you some very helpful insight. Even if you cannot figure out what it is that they are lying about, at the very least, you will detect that they are telling a lie. Ultimately, detecting a lie boils down to trusting your instincts. By knowing the signs to look out for, you may master the art of spotting falsehoods. You can't rely on their body language alone because some people don't give it off at all, so you will need to look at other things that serve as indicators of lying.

• Change in usual body language

If you are analyzing a person's body language to figure out if they are lying to you, first make sure that you know their normal body mannerisms. If you have not acquainted yourself with their usual body language, you won't detect when there is a change. The act of familiarizing yourself with a person's body language is referred to as "baselining" and is vital to detecting a lie. From their handshake to how they stand, there are so many things to learn about a person's usual body mannerisms. When your baseline a person, you can uncover their lies by detecting their honesty signals. Each person you come across has a baseline of what their normal mannerism is. Some people are in a constant state of anxiety and fidgety; they are always pulling their clothes, hair, or whatever—that is normal to them. What you are trying to detect is a switch from this regular behavior. Obviously, there are several reasons why a person might be acting differently from their normal self, and not all reasons point to lying. Still, a change in normal behavior is a vital indicator of lying.

• Constant gesticulation with their non-dominant hand

If you are close with someone, you undoubtedly know their dominant hand—are they left-handed or right-handed? If they start emphasizing their statements with their non-dominant hand while telling you something, this could mean that they are lying. Even though you may force your mouth to lie, the body wants to be honest. However, most people pay attention to the mouth and the words coming out of it rather than the body. To challenge this, the body betrays deception.

• Shifty movements in the face

The face is a major telltale when someone is lying. If someone keeps moving their eyes around while they talk, they are likely lying. Look out for rapid blinking too. On average, an adult blinks between ten and twenty times per minute, but when someone is lying, they may blink upwards of this. Also, pay attention to the direction they look at when they talk. If you know that a person normally looks to the right when trying to remember something, pay attention to where they look when you ask them a question. Chances are they will look to their left to think of an answer quickly. Note that this does not always indicate deception. In some cases, they may have forgotten something, and their mind may be attempting to help them remember.

• Instability in posture

Another indicator of possible deception is if the person keeps rocking back and forth while you converse. This means that they are feeling off-balance. They may also put their weight more significantly on one foot, which results in an asymmetrical posture. Asymmetry indicates a cognitive dissonance between the brain's left and right hemispheres. So, when someone is in that posture, they may be lying. Or, they don't know about the topic being discussed—

which is also a form of lying. Asymmetry may also be exhibited by cocking one's head aside as head-tilting may indicate a lie.

Other things to pay attention to when trying to detect a lie are:

- Vagueness – they offer very little detail about the situation or event.
- They repeat the questions you ask before answering.
- Use sentence fragments with many filler words.
- They don't offer specific details when you challenge their story.
- They appear to be indifferent – shrugging, a bored look, and a lack of facial expression. People do this to avoid conveying emotions or being ousted while they are lying.

The bottom line is that body language can help determine whether a person is lying. However, ensure you pay attention to all the other signals provided above. The fact remains that there is no universally accepted, definitive way to tell when someone is lying. Every hint you get from their body language and the way they deliver their story are clues that might let you know whether they are being honest or not. Therefore, you may sometimes get it wrong. If you fully learn and assimilate the signs to look out for, though, you can become masterful at detecting lies through body language.

Note: The best thing to pay attention to is your immediate instinctual reaction to their story. This often turns out to be more accurate than every other technique. So, do not be quick to discard the feeling in your gut. Most times, it is leading you down the right path to the truth!

Chapter Nine: Dealing with Workspace Manipulators

Sometimes, bosses can make you feel incredibly safe and secure; other times, they make you extremely anxious. You do not know who they really are. You cannot securely share your ideas, thoughts, and opinions without the fear of backlash. On the other hand, there is a coworker that consistently offers to do something for you while making you feel indebted. Nobody seems to be trustworthy in your workplace. So, you are afraid that one day, you might experience a total violation of your privacy by some of the colleagues you trust enough to tell things to.

In a perfect world, your workplace should be like your place of solace—somewhere you can goof around with happy souls while getting quality work in. In this perfect world, you can easily identify the bad and negative people because they have evil costumes that set them apart from the rest of the workers. Unluckily for you, the real world is far from being perfect. You may be a happy employee who is simply content with doing a job you are in love with. You may have coworkers that are just as happy, contented, and positive. However, there are also negative ones. In the workplace, telling good and bad people apart is even harder than it is in your personal life.

Manipulation in the workplace is getting more attention than usual now, yet it is not as widely discussed as manipulation in social and personal relationships. It may be from your boss or coworker— basically anybody that works in the same place as you. Some of your coworkers may seem to support you, give you positive criticism, and cheer you on when you attempt to pull off a joke, all while digging you a big, wide hole to fall into. If you are not careful, you won't figure them out until you have fallen into their hole. What makes coworkers like this dangerous is that they can easily manipulate any situation to make you stand out as the bad person, whereas they are the actual bad guys. These coworkers are psychological manipulators, and knowing how to figure them out can save your career in the long run.

In all the scenarios so far, you can see that you are being manipulated. Unless you know the psychological manipulator's tactics in the workplace, you may not even realize this. Even when you know that you are being manipulated, you may feel too helpless to do anything about it. Before you learn how you can handle emotional and psychological manipulators in the workplace, how do you even identify them?

The first thing to know is that workplace manipulators tend to do things to build your confidence. They may tell you that you are the smartest person they have ever worked with, or that you are their favorite person in the whole company. When a manipulative coworker tells you this, they are subtly telling you that soon, you will become their favorite poodle at work. A narcissistic coworker has a fervent need for admiration and attention from everyone—they feed on the attention. So, when you have a coworker who is always charming to everyone, be wary— such a person might possess the dark triad traits. Manipulators in the workplace are cursorily nice to everyone. They have enough "sweet words" to go around. In the end, they aim to wrap everyone around their fingers. Once they achieve this, they can exploit you however they want, and you won't even recognize it. While not every sensational person is a manipulator, your best bet is to remain grounded no matter what.

Workplace manipulators attempt to destabilize reality as you know it. Has a coworker ever done something unpleasant to you, and when you point it out, they tell you that it is just in your head? That is manipulative behavior. Manipulators want to control the conversation, and the only way they can do that is to shake your reality and make you doubt yourself. This goes back to the gaslighting techniques in Chapter Three. Like classic manipulators, they change your reality to the point where you start doubting yourself and thinking that you have gone mad.

They will project their bad behaviors onto you and shift the blame to you, making you believe that they are only responding to your behaviors. They may ask you if you have ever wondered why they seem to behave badly to you. Questions such as this are attempts at projecting and shifting the blame. A manipulative coworker might say something like, "I am not lazy. I just think that other team members aren't putting in enough effort, and you want to blame me for it." Psychological manipulators will blame everybody else except themselves. The goal is to leave their victims morally contrite. "I would have done a much better job if you hadn't given me a project that is clearly poor in quality. I wish you would be a better manager."

When you engage in arguments with a workplace manipulator, they find ways to digress to irrelevant topics. They do this to win their argument. If you say you do not believe in religion, they might say that means you support a smaller religious group—anything to digress from the topic. They do this to frustrate you to the point where you see no option but to concede to their "superior" argument. If you don't, trust that they can go on with it all day. This sort of classic manipulation tactic is popular with politicians.

Knowing workplace manipulators is one thing; handling them is another.

Below are some tips for you to deal with manipulators at work:

- **Avoid them:** Once you identify that a colleague is manipulative, the best step to take is to stay away from them. Unless it is absolutely necessary, don't interact with them. Staying away from them will make you less likely to fall victim to their manipulative acts.

- **Learn and exercise your rights:** Knowing your rights come in handy when dealing with manipulative people in the workplace or otherwise. Additionally, you should be prepared to defend yourself if you feel like your rights are being violated. Educate yourself on the rights you have in the workplace. Learning and exercising your right is a crucial step to establish boundaries between you and the manipulator.

- **Question them:** Most manipulators don't ask; they demand. They expect you to do whatever it takes to meet their demands. When your workplace manipulator makes such unreasonable demands, ensure you hit them back with the right questions. For example, you can ask them if they consider what they are requesting to be fair. Asking questions pushes them to question their motives for making the demand. As a result, they may back off. Otherwise, they will continue to pester you with demands. In this case, you should use any of the other tactics that have been discussed.

- **Say 'No':** Outrightly tell them no when they make demands. Learning the ability to say no is vital in your interpersonal and professional relationships. If you can't learn to say no, many people will assume that they can take advantage of you and exploit your lack of boundaries. If the manipulative coworker doesn't want to take "no" for an answer, tell them you will report to the HR.

Once you put these tips into use, you will keep away manipulative colleagues and enjoy your workplace more.

Chapter Ten: How NLP is Leveraged to Manipulate Others

Neuro-Linguistic Programming (NLP) is regarded as one of the most prominent mind control techniques in the world. It is used by everyone from politicians to the media and marketing companies. Yet, many people do not believe that NLP is being used as leverage to manipulate other people.

Richard Bandler and John Grinder introduced NLP in the 1970s. Soon, it became a popular concept in the psychoanalytic field, the occult, and the New Age worlds in the '80s. It was not until the '90s and '00s that it became a force in the marketing, advertising, and political world. It has become such an intricate part of advertising and marketing that many people don't even know its use in communication. Nearly everyone in businesses that center on influencing people knows and applies some of the NLP techniques—if not all. Individuals who have mastered NLP can trick people and get them to do things in the most surprising ways.

In case you haven't heard of it before, NLP is a scientific method used to influence or change people's thinking and behaviors to achieved specific outcomes, usually desired ones. For years, NLP has been used as a method for treating anxiety disorders and phobias. It has also been used to improve performance and happiness. All this is done through the use of certain perceptual, communication, and behavioral techniques, making it easier for people to modify their thoughts and actions, usually for the better. NLP focuses on language processing to some extent; however, you should not confuse it with Natural Language Processing, which has the same acronym.

NLP was invented based on the belief that humans operate through internal perceptions of the world they pick up through sensory experiences. Thus, NLP attempts to detect and change unconscious biases and limitations in a person's perception of the world. NLP is quite different from hypnotherapy. Unlike hypnotherapy, NLP uses conscious language to facilitate changes in thinking and behavior.

Simply put, when using NLP, you layer subtle meaning into your spoken and written language to put suggestions into a person's unconscious mind without them realizing. As much as NLP is meant to be a force for good, it is also used as a tool for manipulation. However, it is more about the person using it than the technique itself. The word "manipulation" has a negative connotation, but this doesn't mean that NLP is automatically negative because it is being used for manipulation.

Many NLP techniques can be leveraged to influence or manipulate people. Some of the techniques are:

- Anchoring
- Rapport
- Swish pattern
- Visual-Kinesthetic dissociation

These techniques are taught in a pyramidal structure, with some advanced techniques being taught only in expensive seminars.

How does NLP work? The NLP practitioner starts by closely monitoring the individual they are working to influence or manipulate. They pay attention to subtle body changes and movements, such as pupil dilation, eye movement, skin flush, and nervous tics. By paying attention to these, they can quickly figure out:

- The side of the brain used predominantly by the person
- The predominant sense in their brain
- How their brain acquires, interprets, stores, and use information
- When they are making things up or outrightly lying

One of NLP's central features is the belief that an individual is naturally biased toward one of the five sensory systems. This is known as the Preferred Representational System (PRS). NLP practitioners can quickly detect this bias through their use of language. A phrase such as, "I hear your point" may signify a bias toward the auditory system. That is, people who use this phrase instead of "I see your point" have an auditory PRS. So, an NLP practitioner seeks to identify a person's PRS and then build their change therapy around it.

After monitoring the person's body changes and movements and using it to acquire certain information about them, the NLP practitioners then gradually and subtly recreate the subject's mannerisms, including their body language and how they speak. They start to speak with language patterns that are designed to trigger the person's primary sense to put them in specific emotional states. This is anchoring and rapport all together. The NLP practitioner is doing this to improve communication with the subject and achieve response through empathy. Essentially, the NLP practitioner is faking the person's social cues to get them to become open and responsive to suggestibility.

If the person (subject) has a predominantly visual PRS, the practitioner will use language that targets their visual sense. For example, "Do you see what I mean?" If the person has a predominantly auditory PRS, they will say things like, "Are you listening to this?" or "Hear me out and listen closely." By mirroring the individual's linguistic patterns, the practitioner is attempting to build rapport. Rapport is the mental and psychological state you enter when you let your guard down. You only reach this stage in NLP when you are sure that the person talking with you shares the same mannerism, making you trust them more. As soon as rapport is achieved, the practitioner subtly takes over the interactions without the subject realizing it. Having learned and mirrored their mannerism and language patterns, they can now subtly facilitate changes in the other person's thoughts and behaviors. Combined with an array of other NLP techniques, the practitioner now has the power to steer the other person in whatever direction they want. This is possible as long as the other individual is not conscious of what is going on. From there, this person can convince the subject to do anything—from donating to getting into bed with them.

Normally, you are supposed to seek consent before you practice NLP on people. However, unfortunately, many manipulators are familiar with this technique and know how to use it on you without your knowledge. So, how do you make sure that you are not manipulated through NLP without your knowledge or consent?

- Check to see if they are copying your body language. If you know someone manipulative or into NLP, be wary when you interact with them. Make sure they aren't sitting the same way as you are, or mirroring your hand movements. To test them, make a few movements and see if they recreate them.

- If they pay too much attention to your eyes, make random movements with your eyes and move them in unpredictable patterns.

- Do not allow suspicious people to touch you. When you have a conversation with a manipulative NLP user, and you are in a heightened emotional state, if you allow the personal touch you in that state, they will anchor you. This means they will put you in that same emotional state later, whenever they want.

- Pay attention to their language. The vaguer the language is, the more likely it is to put you in a state of suggestibility. How? You have little to nothing to agree or disagree with.

- Be cautious of people who use permissive language a lot. This is a major technique in NLP. The idea is that the best way to put someone in a suggestive state is by seeking permission to do that thing. "Feel free to sit with me" is an example of a statement that an NLP practitioner will use.

- Read between the lines. The use of language with layered meaning is one of the hallmark NLP techniques. If someone says something like, "Reading, nutrition, and sleep with me are the favorite things to do." This sentence might seem harmless, but there is a layered meaning. Check to see if you can read between the lines and pick up on it!

NLP can be leveraged for manipulation since it is all about altering a person's thinking and behavioral patterns. So, you should always be careful around NLP practitioners. Understand that NLP is regarded as a pseudo-science by the scientific community, so it is best not to use it for anything.

Chapter Eleven: Mind Control and Brain Washing

Have you ever tried to get someone to agree with you on something? Has anyone ever tried to get you to agree with—or even do—something? Certainly, you must have experienced this many times. Everyone is constantly exposed to different persuasion methods, both online and offline, but you don't pay attention to it. Naturally, nobody does. Even though you may think of these things as persuasion or "convincing," psychologists like to refer to them as brainwashing and mind control techniques.

"Brainwashing" was introduced to the public through the work of Edward Hunter, an American journalist who specialized in oriental issues. In Psychology, brainwashing is also referred to as *thought reform*, which is altering or changing a person's thinking pattern. It is as simple as that. Brainwashing, obviously, cannot happen without mind control. After all, how can a person affect and change your thinking patterns if they cannot gain access to your mind? There are many ways through which social influence is achieved. However, brainwashing is the most invasive form of gaining influence. Brainwashing requires the total isolation and dependency of the victim for the manipulator to gain influence.

As a result, this method is commonly used in cults and prison camps. In fact, the term itself originated and became popular during the Korean war when the Korean and Chinese military reportedly captured American soldiers, held them in prison camps, and brainwashed them. After brainwashing, the prisoners apparently confessed to using germs as warfare ammunition, even when they hadn't. At the end of it all, they pledged their allegiance to the communist state of China. After the war, more than twenty-one soldiers refused to return to America even though they had been set free. This is just how deeply brainwashing can go. However, this story poses some questions that skeptics often use in discrediting the effectiveness of brainwashing. If brainwashing was that effective, why did only twenty-one out of over 20,000 prisoners refuse to return to the United States? Doesn't that prove that brainwashing does not work as well as the media portrays it?

Mind control and brainwashing are categorized under social influence. In the world, social influence happens each minute of the day. Someone, somewhere, is always trying to get a friend or acquaintance or stranger to do something. Every day, people use various methods to change other people's beliefs, attitudes, and behaviors. Some people use compliance to initiate change in an individual's behavior without considering the person's attitudes or beliefs. Persuasion is used to initiate a change in attitude. The education method is used to try to change beliefs, which is why it's called the propaganda method.

Comparatively, brainwashing aims to change a person's beliefs, attitudes, and behavior; basically, everything that forms the person's identity and makes them who they are. The brainwasher requires complete control over their victim, including how and what they eat, their sleeping patterns, and every other basic human need. The idea is to completely hijack the victim's identity to the point where they no longer have a sense of identity. Once this happens, the brainwasher introduces them to a different set of behaviors, beliefs, and attitudes that align with the brainwasher's needs.

While many experts believe that it is possible to brainwash an individual under the right situation and condition, some consider it an improbable form of influence. They believe that brainwashing is not achievable without the presence of the fear or threat of physical violence. This means that for brainwashing to be achievable, there has to be coercion, whether physical or nonphysical. However, experts further believe that the effects of brainwashing are transient, regardless of the methods or techniques used. The process of brainwashing doesn't necessarily eradicate a person's identity; rather, it pushes it behind the scenes. Once the brainwasher stops reinforcing the process, the hidden identity starts coming back. This explains why most of the captured American soldiers, despite the torture and reported brainwashing, chose to return to the country, and only a paltry twenty-one actually stayed back.

To brainwash their victims, manipulators follow a series of steps:

- They assault your identity to break you.
- They incite feelings of guilt to make you feel bad about who you are.
- They encourage you to accept their view of who you are to enact self-betrayal.
- Once you are at your breaking point, they offer you a possibility of salvation. They start being lenient and offering to help you.
- They help you confess to everything they have accused you of.
- They channel your guilt to different things, so much so that you become confused about what your original crime is. This leaves you in a blank state, meaning the brainwasher can fill you in with whatever they want.
- They then help you to release your guilt. This is a tactic to get rid of your belief system. Once this is done, they can introduce you to a new set of beliefs.

- Finally, the rebuilding of self—which is all about reconstructing your attitudes, beliefs, and behaviors.

Just like that, the work of a brainwasher is done, and you become an entirely new person with your old self hidden deep beneath the layers of new beliefs.

As noted earlier, mind control is the foundation of successfully brainwashing a person. To use basic mind control on people, individuals with the dark triad traits first try to understand whom they are dealing with. Unsurprisingly, this is such an easy task for them. The first thing they do is to figure out who is vulnerable enough to be exploited. Everyone is vulnerable in one way or another, and psychopaths understand this. So, they seek out specific vulnerabilities in their victims. The more insight they gain into what makes you vulnerable, the easier it is to control and brainwash you. There are three aspects of personality that they understand better than you know.

The first is your *private personality*: your internal experience of yourself. Your private personality covers everything from your thoughts and attitudes to your values, preferences, emotions, ambitions, hopes, and positive traits. It also includes some negative traits that you may try to improve, ignore, or hide from others.

The second is your *public persona*: how you want other people to think of you. It is the part of yourself that you show to others to make them view you in a positive light. You subconsciously try to amplify your good traits and downplay the bad ones.

The third aspect is *reputation*: how people actually see you. No matter how much effort you put into hiding or amplifying your traits, people will always form an impression of their own, usually based on their beliefs, opinions, and values. They use these three things to filter the information they get from you to form their personal perception. This is why some people may describe you as a nice person, while others outrightly say you are unkind. This is the result of the filtering and distortion of information.

An important thing to note here is that the first impression is formed quite quickly, usually within a few seconds of meeting. As time moves by, people then subconsciously seek out information to confirm their initial impression. Even when they see the information that contradicts their opinions and perceptions, they tend to ignore it. This is a natural human bias. So, if you like someone the first time you meet them, they become likable by the day. Likeability is one of the major weapons manipulators and brainwashers use to influence and subsequently dominate. The more you like someone, the likelier you are to be influenced by them.

So, how do people with dark triad traits use this information? When a dark triad persona meets you for the first time, they immediately assess you for possible usability and value. Then, they proceed to assess your personality. Your face, word, and body language are all they need to get a hint of who you are. Based on what they find out, they begin to project a persona that empathizes with yours; they do this to form an intimate bond with you. Once the bond is established, manipulating, brainwashing, and mind-controlling become very straightforward. The manipulator seeks out your strengths, weaknesses, insecurities, needs, and things you value the most. When they talk to you, there are four vital things they are trying to convey:

- I like who you are.
- I am just like you. We are the same.
- I can keep your secrets.
- I am the perfect person (friend, partner, lover, companion) that you need.

The thing about mind control is that the person may not follow the techniques in a sequence; they may overlap or jump from one technique to another. Yet, they can successfully influence your decision-making process. What distinguishes mind control from brainwashing is the perception of the manipulator by the person being manipulated. In brainwashing, the manipulator is sometimes an obvious enemy—someone you don't like. But what most people fail to note is that you can also be brainwashed by someone you consider a friend. In fact, brainwashing is much easier when you are close to the manipulator. You believe that someone is your friend, teacher, and they have your best interests at heart. Unknowingly, you become a willing participant in the mind control and brainwashing process. As mentioned earlier, the manipulator tries to get four important messages across when trying to get you to open up. The aim of passing this message is to deceive you into believing they are a friend.

The first message is, "*I like who you are.*" Everyone wants to be liked. It is basic human nature to want to be noticed, admitted, and accepted by others. Consciously or subconsciously, you seek compliments from others. It is normally flattering when someone notices you and actually pays attention to you. Narcissists and psychopaths understand this basic human need, so they exploit it. They tell you things that make you feel good about yourself—making you feel accepted and understood. This is why they are always so superficially charming; however, you may not realize that the charms and niceties are fake.

The second message is, "*I am exactly like you.*" Based on what the psychopaths now know about you, both from their assessment and what you let on, they begin to share details of their own life that corroborate with yours. You start to believe that they are letting their guard down. Unknown to you, most times, it is all lies and vague tales. Because the information they share aligns with your values, the bond you feel with them becomes stronger.

The third message is, "*I can keep your secrets.*" Since the manipulator appears to be sharing "intimate" details of their life, you easily let your guard down and start telling them more about yourself. After all, you feel secure, and they seem to understand you on a deeper level. So, what is not to share? What you don't know is that this manipulator is fulfilling your psychological desire for security and safety, which is all they need to suck you in further. The more information you give to them, the better they can project a person that appears to be a perfect match for yours.

Eventually, you will come to accept the fourth message, which is that the manipulator "*is the perfect companion for you.*" They now have a strong reputation in your mind, and they feel special to your heart. The manipulator has achieved their goal, and you are now bonded with them. Depending on whether you can snap out of the sunken place or not, your fate may be forever linked to your manipulator.

You probably think that these things are basic things that happen in a "normal" relationship. True, but only if the manipulator did not have an ulterior motive and fake their persona. The manipulator approached you for a reason, and once they get what they want, they will move on to their next victim.

Mind control and brainwashing are all about power and control. Relationships formed with mind control techniques tend to have a power imbalance, and the power is always with the manipulator. That is the ultimate objective: to gain and exert power and control over others.

Chapter Twelve: Media Manipulation and Subliminal Influencing

Media is all about influence. Everything you see in the media is designed to influence you. However, have you ever wondered if the media is also manipulating you? Some believe that the media is more a tool of manipulation than influence. What if these people are "on to something," as they say on social media? According to Wikipedia, media manipulation is "a series of related techniques in which partisans create an image or argument that favors their particular interests." Basically, the media can create a certain perception of an issue, a person, a group, or anything to the public. The public would believe it because the media is supposed to be the ultimate source of factual information. The media does this through the use of subliminal messages.

Anybody that consumes media content is susceptible to media manipulation and subliminal influencing. For years, subliminal messages have been regarded as one of the dark arts used in persuasion and manipulation. Advertisers, marketers, politicians, and the media are believed to use subliminal messages to manipulate and modify people's behaviors. But how effective are media manipulation and subliminal influencing? Do subliminal messages actually work?

The concept of subliminal messages was first introduced to the public around the 1950s. Since then, researchers have sought to understand the concept more. In the last 60 years, the scientific understanding of subliminal messages has matured.

"Subliminal" means "below the threshold." Subliminal messages are regarded as signals that are below the absolute threshold level of your consciousness. In other words, they are messages that you cannot consciously pick up on because they are targeted at your subconscious and unconscious awareness. Even if you actively lookout for a subliminal signal, you cannot actively pick up on them. The absolute threshold is the lowest level of stimuli you can detect, whether auditory, visual, or sensory. When a stimulus from your external environment falls below the absolute threshold, you cannot detect it consciously.

It is believed that the media subliminally influences consumers' perceptions by deliberately using communication techniques that are engineered to generate specific responses. The aim is to get people to do things that they ordinarily would not do. In short, both the perception and response to subliminal influencing happen in the subconscious mind. The two attributes must be clearly defined because the popular misconception is about supraliminal influencing. Supraliminal, although confused for subliminal, is quite different. While both subliminal and supraliminal messages evoke neural responses that subsequently influence thoughts and behaviors, supraliminal messages are perceivable by the conscious mind. Your conscious awareness can perceive when receiving supraliminal signals, but it cannot perceive subliminal ones.

How does subliminal influencing work? The mind comprises of two parts: the conscious and subconscious mind. The conscious mind gives you executive control of your mind. You can think, feel, judge, and experience in full awareness mode at the conscious level.

On the other hand, the subconscious mind is the part of your mind that is below the level of conscious awareness. It is the hiding place for your motives, desires, and past experiences. The fascinating thing about the subconscious mind is that it operates on autopilot. When it comes to information processing, your subconscious mind is much more powerful than your consciousness. The subconscious can process 20,000 bytes of information simultaneously, while the consciousness can only handle three to seven bytes. Throughout the day, you breathe in and breathe out. But are you consciously aware of every breath you take? Are you aware of every step you take and how you avoid falling? No, because all these things are done subconsciously. That is how subconscious thinking and processing occurs. Subliminal messages are targeted at the subconscious mind.

Modern science says that there are seven categories of sensory input:

- Visual – sight
- Auditory – hearing
- Tactile – touch
- Olfactory – taste
- Gustatory – smell
- Vestibular – balance and movement
- Proprioception – body awareness

Among these seven, the visual and auditory senses are the most prominent, which is why they are also the ones that subliminal messages are targeted at.

Visual subliminal messages in the media are either sub-visual or embedded. Sub-visual cues are flashed very quickly in media content, so quickly that you cannot perceive them. Embedded messages are static visuals in plain sight, with an unchanging environment. They are often used in advertisements. An example is the dollar bill in some KFC burger ads. Auditory subliminal messages are either subaudible or backmasking. Subaudible messages have low-volume sound inserted into high-volume audios, such that you cannot hear them. Backmasking is a visual-audio message recorded in reverse so that the actual message is hidden when it is played forward.

Now, how exactly do these messages influence your behavior? One of the theories proposed is that the subliminal priming works to distribute activation in the semantic network. Humans have semantically connected links of concepts in the brain, and each concept exists in a bigger network of interconnected concepts. Take Microsoft as an example: When prompted about Microsoft, you will probably think of Bill Gates, computers, windows, etc. Microsoft is often associated with innovation. So, if you were to briefly flash a Microsoft logo to someone and then ask them to complete a task, they are likely to be more innovative in their approach because their subconscious has picked up on what Microsoft is associated with.

Because subliminal messages are targeted at your subconscious so that an advertiser, politician, and other people can influence you to do things that you ordinarily may not agree to do, they count as a form of manipulation. This explains why people think that the media is all-powerful. They understand the power the media has and how they use that power. Media manipulation and subliminal influencing should be considered unethical and treated as such because they perfect the art of exploiting a person's unawareness.

Chapter Thirteen: The Dark Psychology of Cyberspace

The Internet has become a safe space for narcissists, psychopaths, Machiavellians, and people that generally have one dark trait or another—it is somewhere they can find and pick their victims. Internet users refer to these people as "trolls." Still, they do not seem to understand the damage that these personalities can cause. In fact, "trolling" is the Internet's lighthearted way of simplifying these personalities' acts. Trolling is an act of disrupting and upsetting conversations on the Internet just to evoke certain responses from people. When trolls comment, you can tell that they have no other purpose for doing this except to upset everyone else. Trolls lie, deceive, exaggerate, and purposely say offensive things to negatively tip others' emotional states. As much as you may want to disregard it, it is evident that these people pollute cyberspace and make it more and more inhabitable for normal humans. If you thought narcissists and their counterparts are hard to identify in real life, you should try the Internet.

The dark psychology of cyberspace is a metaphorical and conceptual framework used to define a virtual world where all criminal, deceptive, malevolent, deviant, and harmful activities are being committed in an abstract space. Various cyber platforms, such as social networking sites, forums, blogs, and chatrooms, provide an ideal environment for narcissists, psychopaths, sadists, and Machiavellians to reinforce that need to put others in possible harm to advance their interests. These dark personalities are taking different forms online. Some of them are social media influencers, bloggers, and other people that have the power to influence the behaviors of their followers and possibly even manipulate them into doing certain things. Research confirms that narcissism is a rapidly-increasing tendency for most people on the Internet. More and more Internet users are feeling self-important with a disturbingly disproportionate ego. The Internet is their paradise, but what is it *exactly* about cyberspace that makes people increasingly dark?

The Internet can be considered an abstract space. On the Internet, anybody can assume whatever image they want. They can even choose to be anonymous. Due to the sense of anonymity that the Internet offers, and the ability to create whatever perception you want, many dark personalities have turned social media networks and the likes into their haven. Add that to the lack of physical interactions and minimal effort input, and you will understand why the cyberspace has become the place for trolls and predators.

Recently, psychologists have put resources into finding the relationship that exists between the dark side in humans and the dark side of the Internet. What did they find? They found that certain online activities have a direct connection to different personality traits. The most prominent traits being Narcissism, Machiavellianism, Sadism, and Spitefulness. The result of the studies conducted suggested that all of these four traits correspond to how engaged people are with online activities.

Narcissism is an excessive preoccupation with oneself and with social media. Narcissists cannot get enough of the Internet and its many wonders, including social networking sites, such as Twitter, Facebook, YouTube, etc. Machiavellianism correlates directly with online gambling, online dating, online gaming, and online sex.

Basically, people who are excessively engaged with these online activities are likely Machiavellians in real life. Sadism correlates with online gaming and online sex. Spitefulness correlates with online shopping, online gaming, and online sex.

This is not to imply that everyone on the Internet is a raging sadist or spiteful person. The research points out that these dark personality traits are associated with higher-than-usual engagement with specific online activities, which points to a sort of psychological affinity for those activities. For example, if someone uses Instagram more regularly than the average person—almost to the point of obsession—they may be narcissistic. This is because Instagram is the perfect social media for narcissists to showcase their "superiority" to others. However, it has nothing to do with quantity. Early studies on the Internet and social media use have shown that, to some extent, psychologically dark people use the Internet differently from everybody else. For example, sadists tend to use their Twitter profiles to "troll" celebrities and other people. There have been examples of some so-called trolls wishing people who disagree with them insufferable pain.

In some cases, they simply rain a barrage of demeaning insults on another person. Fat-shaming, slut-shaming, wealth-shaming, and many acts are perpetrated by trolls online. While not all trolls are sadists, the possibility that a high number of these trolls are sadistic to some extent cannot be dispelled.

Some psychologists have suggested that the amount of time you spend online can increase your dark personality traits. According to research by the Stanford University School of Medicine, regular Internet usage can increase one's impulsivity and online shopping. Considering the research findings, it wouldn't be a "reach" to hypothesize that the time one spends online can nurture certain personality traits that are considered dark, e.g., narcissism.

Recently, Canadian researchers, namely Professor Eric Buckels, Paul Trapnell, and Delroy Paulhus, decided to find out the kind of people trolls are. So, they conducted two virtual tests with 1,200 participants. In the tests, they gave all the participants personality tests to complete and a survey about their commenting behavior on the Internet. In 2014, the result of this study was published in the September issue of *Personality and Individual Differences.* The study aimed to find if there was anything that linked trolling to the dark triad traits. In the end, the researchers found that the dark triad traits were higher among those who highlighted trolling as their favorite online activity.

So, it is safe to say that online activities are attractive to people who already have soaring dark trait levels. It is also okay to conclude that spending extensive time in cyberspace can increase dark traits levels. The next time you come across a troll online, keep in mind that the best thing you can do is ignore them.

Chapter Fourteen: The Dark Psychology of Cults

Cult activity is something that is frequently seen on TV and is just as common in society. Cults have this ability to capture people's attention, and the leader(s) of a cult can be anybody. However, there is a pattern to them. You might have wondered how a single person can influence so many people? Well, it all boils down to manipulation, mind control, gaslighting, and brainwashing.

If you wonder how people fall victim to the allure of cults, the first thing you should know is that it is human nature to seek comfort wherever one can find it. So, in this world where you cannot vouch for anybody to have your back, many people turn to cults to get the comfort they desire. Cults promote an illusion, which is why they are attractive to many people. Cult leaders have been known to make realistically unattainable promises. They sell lofty dreams that are not offered by any other group in society. Some cults may tell you that they will help you achieve a level of success that has never been seen before—something no one else can promise you. Some of the things they promise include financial security, complete health, and even eternity. These very things are at the core of human desires.

The world today is a tough one. More abstract issues are taking over the scene. Nothing seems to be black and white anymore. As a result, a lot of people are confused, and they want clarity—to the point where they will seek it anywhere they can get it. Cults offer absolute clarity to everything these people want to know. Many people join cults because they genuinely believe that they would get absolute answers to their questions. Cult leaders position themselves as having answers to questions, such as life vs. death, good vs. evil, politics, meaning, and religion. They promote messages that seem straightforward and sensible—the opposite of everything humans face in everyday life. But when you look in hindsight, you will discover that these seemingly simple answers and solutions are as vague as they come.

When people think of cults, they subconsciously assume that only malicious people join cults. It comes as a surprise when they learn that most cult members are ordinary people. They can come from any background, tax bracket, or zip code. Nevertheless, there is a pattern with these people regardless of their background: poor self-esteem. Cult leaders tend to target their messages toward people with poor self-identity and even poorer self-esteem. This is because people with self-esteem problems are easier to gaslight, manipulate, and brainwash. When someone is in a state where they constantly look for their identity in other people, they are vulnerable to cult leaders and other manipulative personalities because they offer supportive and validating environments.

Although some cults may seem helpful to their followers, it is crucial to note that most of them are destructive. They use different manipulative techniques to establish and maintain control over their members. This makes the members remain committed to the activities of the cult. Thought reforms, coercive persuasion, and brainwashing are some of the popular techniques used.

The takeaway is that cult leaders are masters of mind control. They effortlessly convince their members to isolate themselves from everyone that matters to them (gaslighting), retract from society, and give up their possessions for the cult's benefit. They use public humiliation, self-incrimination, paranoia, and other established techniques to maintain dominance over their members. It is hard to give a specific reason why people form cults. Still, one reasonable thing that is common to everyone who use manipulative tactics and techniques to advance their self-interests is the need to assert power, control, and dominance over others.

The psychological effects cults leave on their victims can be damaging. One thing about people who join cults is that they do not know they are in a cult until they are out of it. While it may be obvious to those around them, victims don't recognize the significance and symbolism of what they have become a part of. Most members enter a cult willingly without understanding the impact and power it could hold over them. This is because they tend to pay more attention to the perceived benefits more than the possible dangers. Once they are out, victims of cults often spend years trying to overcome and repair the emotional, mental, and psychological damage incurred during their time in the cult.

Finally, many people think of cults as religious, but this is a misconception. Cults can be political, philosophical, business-related, and lifestyle-inclined. An example of a lifestyle cult is the Hare Krishna cult, where the members adopted the Eastern lifestyle, wearing Eastern-themed dressing, easting Eastern cuisine, and embracing the meditation practices from the East.

Chapter Fifteen: Examples of Political Propaganda

Propaganda is defined as the dissemination of information, factual or otherwise, to influence public opinion. Breaking it down further, propaganda is a cohesive and systematic effort to influence or outrightly manipulate people's opinions, beliefs, attitudes, and actions through the use of symbolism. This symbolism is portrayed utilizing gestures, words, banners, insignia, hairstyles, postage stamps, etc. Propaganda can be based on assumptions, half-truths, arguments, rumors, or lies. Political propaganda is basically the same thing but in a political sense.

Propagandists have an intentional set of goals they seek to achieve. To achieve their goals, they deliberately handpick information that is both subjective and objective and then proceed to present them in ways that can have a ripple effect on the consumers of that information. To maximize the effect, they may distort or omit the most vital parts of the information—or lie. Propagandists work to divert the attention of the public from everything except their agenda. Propaganda is often described as misleading or biased because it usually tells one side of the story to promote a certain image or outlook. Political propaganda is real and is even more obvious on social media these days. From Twitter to Facebook, you can most certainly always see a post promoting a certain view or cause.

The general consensus is that propaganda has been around for many years, probably from the start of time. In fact, what the snake did to Eve in the Garden of Eden can be considered as propaganda. For centuries, humans have used propagandist principles to manipulate public perception and opinion. However, the term itself was not introduced until the seventeenth century. Propaganda, contrary to what you may think, is not just used in politics; it can be used in several aspects of life, including public relations, diplomatic negotiations, collective bargaining, commercial advertising, and political campaigns. Some people believe that Obama's "CHANGE" campaign of 2008 is an ideal example of NLP-style propaganda. Regardless of the field, propaganda has no specific or definitive target audience. It can be targeted toward any group of people at a local, national, international, and global level.

There are different examples of propaganda. Advertisements are generally considered as propaganda because they seek to promote a particular product or service. For instance, a Pepsi advertisement promotes Pepsi drinks as the best. Some glaring ads even shade any other drink that is considered a competitor, such as Coca-Cola.

Focusing specifically on political propaganda, it might interest you that political propaganda has been around for as long as thes written language—several examples in history date back to the earliest civilization in human history. At the start of the seventeenth century, a new religious ideology referred to as Protestantism was tempting and winning over converts from the Catholic Church. However, this was not the only problem the Church had to deal with—many problems were coming from the New World. Fortunately for the Church, the majority of the Western part of the New World were under colonization by Church-backed Monarchs, so the Pope decided to take decisive action. The Pope founded a new papal department that would convert people of the New World to the Catholic faith. This new department was declared the *Congregatio de Propaganda Fide,* meaning "Congregation for Propagating the Faith." This is regarded as the origin of the word "Propaganda." The new creation of the Church sent its missionaries to the New World to share materials used to induct colonists and indigenes to the Catholic faith. These materials were called propaganda then, but no negative connotation was assigned to the word.

At the start of World War I, many of the world governments created offices devoted specifically to creating and sharing propaganda, which was when the word took on a negative connotation to the public. For example, Germany created its Central Office for Foreign Services, dedicated to responding to propaganda shared by the British government. Every material created and distributed by the different nations' propaganda offices was clearly shared to circulate falsified information among the people abroad. However, some of the propaganda materials were actually shared to garner support for the war efforts at home. But the first group to integrate issues regarding war, family, rebellion, obedience, and morality in political propaganda in the most innovative way was the Bolsheviks of Russia. They used propaganda so much so that they could influence the way other governments viewed the use of propagative materials to sway public opinion. The propagandas had such heavy symbolic and emotional meaning that they were able to incite and elicit powerful emotions and reactions, resulting in political unrest. However, political propaganda was not fully embraced until the second World War, where governments across the world were all fighting tooth and nail to achieve their goals.

Adolf Hitler understood the power of symbols and slogans, and how they can be used to motivate people. Hitler established the Ministry of Public Enlightenment and Propaganda in 1933 when he took control of Germany. The United States, Britain, Germany, and Japan all produced tons of ads, posters, images, and similar materials that demonized the enemies and victimized them. They also used propaganda to demand nationalistic allegiance from the citizens, almost to the point of fanaticism.

Since then, propaganda has taken a much more modern approach. Media departments of every political party set up a task force to create propaganda for their campaigns. This is especially evident when it comes to candidate campaigns. Modern propagandists employ several techniques to appeal to emotions. Thankfully, propaganda isn't as manipulative as NLP; however, NLP techniques can be infused in propagandist campaigns. You can easily figure out if something is propaganda by taking a step back and carefully examining and analyzing it.

An interesting example of propaganda can be found in the autobiography of *Jang Jin-Sung,* a former State Poet for the Republic of North Korea. In his autobiography, Jang explained that his job as the national Poet Laureate and member of the inner circle was to write books and reports by "South Koreans," stating that they were frightened and desperate to reconcile with the North. These books and reports were then smuggled into South Korea. Afterward, North Korean spies would sneak the materials into the public. Once they were revealed to the public, the government's claims that South Koreans were scared and eager to reconcile became proven. This awakened and strengthened the spirit of nationalism in North Korea citizens who had no idea that the government faked reports and books. This is a powerful example of how political propaganda can influence and manipulate public opinion and reactions.

In the modern political sphere, some of the ways that propaganda is used include:

- **Taglines, slogans, and catchphrases**: These are short, brief, and catchy words or phrases that are not only easy to process but also easy to remember. Referred to as bite-sized tags, they are usually very powerful enough to incite a mob. They have become increasingly popular thanks to the social media age, where all you need are 120 characters to spread propaganda. Because of how easy they are to share and relay, bite-sized tags are being used for viral propaganda.

 • **Fear-mongering and scapegoating**: This is a singularly powerful propaganda technique that has been around for a long time. Fear-mongering involves using deep and symbolic ideas to sway public opinions by triggering a strong, sometimes irrational, feeling of fear. It is often used alongside scapegoating, which involves blaming a particular group for the problems in society. The two methods are regularly used by racist, xenophobic, discriminatory, and authoritarian groups, political parties, or political candidates.

 • **Demonization**: This involves the characterization of a political opponent as evil, dangerous, and vile in the mind of the public. If used rightly, propaganda can trigger visceral feelings of disgust and fear for the target. This kind of propaganda employs the use of exaggerative and hyperbolic imagery. It is used for the "political smear campaign." If you use social media regularly, you will come across this type of propaganda.

 • **Common folks**: Political candidates use this propaganda technique to get the common people to feel like they directly relate to the propaganda's meaning and message. They do this by using certain colloquialism and symbolism that may seem mundane to the general public. This particular technique is becoming increasingly popular in the United States.

There are several other propaganda techniques which include, *Paternalism, Band-wagoning, Flag waving, Ad Nauseum, Inevitable victory,* and others.

Detecting the fine line between information and propaganda is becoming y harder, making more people susceptible to its psychology. This new age is certainly for propaganda, especially in politics across the virtual and digital sphere. It is important to pay attention to the information you glean online. Know where information comes from and look out for the origin of the information to avoid bias. While you cannot realistically avoid propaganda—it is always in your face—you can ensure that you understand the techniques which propagandists use to persuade, influence, and incite people. This is crucial if you want to maintain your awareness in a world where there is always someone constantly looking to influence you in ways that you may not expect!

Chapter Sixteen: How to Protect yourself from Manipulators

Protecting yourself from manipulators is easy—as long as you are willing to learn how. This may seem like an odd thing to say. After all, why would you not be willing to learn how to protect yourself from predators that could possibly harm you and jeopardize your life? Naturally, everyone's instinct should be to find ways of protecting themselves from manipulative and deceptive individuals. Interestingly, though, some people subconsciously seek out manipulative people, or, more specifically, narcissists, sadists, psychopaths, etc. This happens due to a range of factors.

When Ted Bundy was apprehended and convicted, there were still those who genuinely believed in the possibility of salvaging his soul. These are the kind of people who subconsciously seek to form relationships with narcissists, psychopaths, and so forth. Codependents are an example of people who subconsciously seek out relationships with narcissists. As stated, protecting yourself from individuals with dark triad traits is fairly straightforward when you know what to do. Once you have identified someone that falls into this category in your life, here are some steps you can take to protect yourself from them before they even have the chance to attempt anything.

Stop seeking approval from others

Do not let people define you. Knowingly or unknowingly, many people who fall victim to narcissists or Machiavellians, and their counterparts, are people who seek validation and acceptance from others. This may be funny to you—as narcissists seek approval from people—but the difference is that they don't make it evident. Unless you are familiar with narcissists, you can meet one and not even recognize them. All you will think is that you want to be as confident as they are, not knowing that confidence is a sham. The only way people can manipulate you is if you give them an opening. And the easiest way to give them the opening they seek is to need their approval and validation. Do not pay attention to the four messages they are trying to convey to you. Understand their manipulative ploy for what it is.

Set healthy boundaries and enforce them

Setting boundaries is one thing, but making proactive efforts to enforce those boundaries is another. What do you not want to tolerate from your manipulator? Think about it and decide to stop allowing them to get away with those behaviors. If you are already in a relationship with a manipulator, and do not know how to set healthy boundaries, don't be afraid to seek professional help. Go to therapy and learn how you can establish and stick to the boundaries you set. One of the reasons people with dark personality traits can exploit their victims is because the victims don't set boundaries. And when they do have boundaries, these are exceptionally poor and ineffective. A boundary lets your partner know what you are willing to live with and what you are willing to accept—or do for them.

Pay attention to your vulnerabilities

Before a manipulator uses your vulnerabilities against you, take charge of your story. Everyone has one or more vulnerabilities. Contrary to what manipulative individuals will have you believe, vulnerability isn't a sign of weakness. Instead of letting them use your vulnerabilities against you, find ways to manage them. If you tend to self-blame or self-criticize yourself, seek help from those who make up your support system. For example, your tendency may be overly sympathetic to people. Sympathetic people are more vulnerable to perverse appeals from malicious people. So, be careful and don't allow anybody to take advantage of your sympathetic nature. Studies show that empaths (empathic people) are more susceptible to relationships with a power imbalance, specifically relationships with narcissists.

Establish a support base for yourself

If you don't already have one, establish a circle of supportive and knowledgeable people to make you feel safer and secure. Manipulators tend to isolate their victims, but this is much harder when the victim has supportive friends and family that they are attached to. A pattern with victims of manipulation is that they tend to be people who don't have loved ones around. An example is a college girl in a new city. With nobody to turn to, they tend to fall prey to the manipulator's charm easily. So, form a circle of trusted and loyal friends. Talk to them about your problems. Their insight may be valuable in getting you out of any situation that could potentially harm your mental, emotional, and psychological health.

Constantly remind yourself of your priorities

When you lose yourself to a manipulative person, you lose track of your personal goals and priorities. Manipulators only care about themselves; they will use you to advance their goals while you remain in a static position. They will tell you all sorts of things to discredit your dream and ambition. Even if they don't discredit it, they may try to convince you to change it to something that would be more beneficial to them. Every day, clarify your goals and priorities to yourself. Remind yourself of your dream and ambition. Ask yourself what the tasks you engage in mean to you and how they contribute to your aspirations. If they don't appear to contribute in any way, drop them and start engaging actively in the ones that matter. This is to fortify yourself to an extent where you can't be manipulated into shifting course. You also need the focus to avoid getting too emotionally invested if the manipulator is creating relationship difficulties.

Call it as you see it

One of the reasons why manipulators perpetuate their negative and damning behavior is because they believe that they can't get caught. Sometimes, when you identify that the person you are in a relationship with is manipulative, don't just move on from the relationship. Confront them and let them understand that you know who they are. This will take them aback and shake up their superficial confidence. Wobble up their delusional state of mind in an unavoidable confrontation and let them know *exactly* what you have observed and how their actions affect you. If anything, the manipulator, in this case, will be the one to run far away from you. Before you confront them, though, ensure you have a list of specific offenses, with the minutest and most obvious details. Without the use of specificity, the manipulator may slip through your hands. However, go about it diplomatically rather than rudely.

What are the things you shouldn't do?

- Don't believe the promises of a manipulator; they are false.
- Don't confide in them at all, except for the most basic and mundane things.
- Don't think that you can outsmart or outmaneuver them; they are the experts.
- Don't believe their words, actions, and behaviors to be reflective of your self-worth.

By following these tips, you can take control away from a manipulator and stay in charge of your life.

Conclusion

You have come to the end of an amazing learning journey, and hopefully, it was worth it. Having reached this part of the book, you have successfully unraveled the art of manipulation and the psychology of manipulators.

Right from the start, the book delved deep into dark psychology and the manipulative aspect of it. Consequently, the tempo remained the same as you learned more about mind control and brainwashing techniques such as gaslighting, NLP, subliminal influencing, and so on.

You have learned enough to start protecting yourself from narcissists, psychopaths, Machiavellians, and sadists without question. Never forget that a person can only influence you to the extent you allow them.

The power remains with you always!

Part 2: How to Analyze People

The Little-Known Secrets to Speed Reading a Human, Analyzing Personality Types and Applying Behavioral Psychology

Introduction

What if I told you that you've just made one of the best decisions of your life by reading this book? Well, that's what is happening! If there is one thing successful, powerful people understand about the game of life, it's that life is about people. Scratch that — it's about understanding how the human mind works.

Fortunately, like any skill, you can learn how to analyze people and read people quickly.

Why should you want to learn? Well, it's not all about just influencing people — although if you did pick up this book to learn that, then it is on you to use what you learn for the right reasons, *and not to foster hate.* When you know how to analyze people, you are in a relevant position in society, in that you'll always know how to foster harmony wherever you go.

You know how to get grown adults (who are hollering at each other) to shut up, sit down, and find the similarities in their seemingly different views. You also know how to get your three-year-old to eat their broccoli, even if they're not totally in love with the unpopular veggie.

In this book, we will talk about how you can scientifically analyze people as you interact with them. You will learn to read their body language and the meaning back of the words they say. You'll get a handle on their mannerisms. You're not going to get a certificate for human behavioral psychology by reading this, but by the end of this book, you will understand what it's all about. You will learn and see in others (or yourself) how psychology comes to play in our daily lives in ways that are obvious – and not quite as obvious.

No two individuals are exactly alike — except perhaps those spooky twins from that popular horror movie. So, it matters that you learn about the basic types of human personality, and how you can connect with each. You'll learn what unique gifts these personalities bring to the table. Even more, you will learn how to weave your different personality with another's so you can both work and live together in harmony, experiencing mutual benefit from each other.

How is this book different? There are lots of books out there on the same topic, but this one is up-to-date, without fancy words you have to keep Googling, and there are useful, practical methods you can apply right away to your daily life.

Whether you're reading this book because you want a better love life or you want to be a better friend or colleague, again, you've made the right choice. Once you're finished, you will find that you're much better at observing things you'd have missed before. You'll be able to read people with as much ease as you're reading the words on this very page!

No matter the situation you're faced with, whether bad or good, you'll know how to handle it a lot better, maintaining an objective viewpoint. This results in better relationships, and ultimately, a higher quality of life. Isn't that something we could all use?

Now, let's begin.

Chapter One: The Benefits of Analyzing Others

What does it mean to analyze someone? It's not about squinting your eyes just so and trying to see through to their dark, twisted soul. The human behavioral analysis involves trying to make sense of the chaos that is the way the human mind works. It's about understanding not just what we think about, but why we have the habits of thought and behavior that we do. It's about understanding the way that these thoughts affect our daily choices, both the deliberate ones and the not-so-deliberate ones.

It's about the science (and art) of psychoanalysis, which you can thank Sigmund Freud for. "Psychoanalysis" is derived from the Greek words psykhé which means "soul," and análysis, which means "investigate." You might say it involves a sort of soul-peering.

There are several schools of thought with psychoanalysis, from Freud to Jung. This book isn't about getting into all that detail. You want to learn to read people, and that's what we shall focus on.

How Psychologists Analyze You

So, your buddy Siobhan is a clinical psychologist. You've always wondered if you need to have your guard up around her. Finally –

and courageously – at a party with friends, you ask her, "Hey Siobhan! Are you always analyzing me?"

Well, if she was honest, she'd tell you that yes, she is analyzing you. However, she isn't. Let's get into this ultra-confusing answer I've given you. The job of a clinical psychologist is to pay attention to behaviors, mannerisms of speech, and irregular actions.

Let's say that Siobhan sees someone acting weirdly, saying some really out-there things, then she will definitely take interest and analyze the heck out of them. It's not because she's trying to be a creep, but because she's been trained to analyze behavior. So, even if she wasn't actively analyzing you at that moment, she's analyzing you now, because you've brought her attention to you. She might be wondering how many martinis you've pounded back, whether you're under the influence of something else, or you're simply experiencing an episode of mania.

Now, here's why she says she *isn't trying* to read you. She could do a cold read if she wanted to, but from a professional standpoint, the only way to get a grasp on what you're thinking and feeling is to ask you questions. Go figure.

Often, people seek the help of a clinical psychologist when they're facing some challenge in their relationships, at work, or when things are just not going the way they feel they should. Naturally, the professional psychologist won't just do a cold read. They will ask you questions before they diagnose whatever it is you're troubled by (depression, anxiety, bipolar disorder, and so on).

Even then, the diagnosis is only the start. It gives Siobhan a context for the challenges you're facing and gives her a clue of the treatments you'll need. However, it does little for letting her know the reason you're experiencing these issues or how she can give you a designer treatment for your case.

The psychologist must go even deeper. They'll have some analyzing to do, often covering these aspects:

Origins: They could discuss what growing up was like for you so they can see where the start of your issues lies. They'll want to know about any genetic disorders, what your childhood and family were like, anything of significance that happened to you as a kid, and things of that nature.

Accelerants: These are the changes you might have recently experienced that has caused these problems to surface or made them even worse than usual.

Mechanisms: These cause your issues to happen. The mechanism is literally that: A machine, built from your origins, fueled by your accelerants so that when turned on, they instantly cause these problems of yours to go from zero to ninety in half a millisecond.

Let's look at this in action. Say you have issues with loneliness, underdeveloped social skills, physical, and social anxiety. Those are the problems.

The origins of the problems could be that your family has a history of anxiety, and you never got out much. You only ever spent time with your family, so you didn't learn the basics of getting to know others or communicating with others.

Now let's look at the mechanisms of your possibly fictional anxiety issues. Anxiety is a condition that mostly affects the social sphere of life, surfacing only when you're involved in social situations. Because of this, you make a point of staying away from Thanksgiving dinner, because you just can't handle it. Because of your inability to say hello (like a regular person) to the people around you, you develop a view about yourself that you're "weird."

What accelerates these problems you have? You probably had something trigger depression in you when you were in high school, and since then, you've constantly been worried about your issues getting even worse — and they do, inevitably. I should clarify that this example is oversimplified. Humans are complex. It's not easy to find precisely one reason for why we do the things we do.

One-Tenth of a Second

When you meet someone, you unconsciously and immediately form an impression about them based on your preconceptions of life and the patterns people should conform to. Anecdotally, it takes a little under a minute to size someone up. But the brilliant psychologists at Princeton have studied this phenomenon thoroughly and have found it takes a whopping one-tenth of a second to form your first opinion about someone while relying mostly on body language.

So, what happens after that first impression has been made? Well, every other impression is still mostly based on nonverbal communication. Dr. Albert Mehrabian, in his wonderful book *Silent Messages*, suggests that all that chit-chat and banter between you and the other person only makes up a grand total of 7 percent of all communication you share. The rest of it is from nonverbal cues (body language and facial expressions), and vocal cues.

Because of all this, the question then becomes, how good are you at reading other people, really? If you miss out on the remaining 93 percent of the communication equation, then chances are you're not that great at figuring others out. No worries. You're going to learn how to do that in this book.

Why You Should Learn to Read People

It doesn't matter what profession you're in, or your status in life. The ability to read others around you is a skill with unparalleled benefits. It's like a superpower!

Say you're a radio presenter, and you've been given a script to work with as you interview some businessperson or celebrity. You could be very efficient about your job, sticking to the script, never deviating. That's great! But, what if you could read people?

You'd be able to tell when your guest has a lot more to say on a certain subject, go off script, and get some new angle no one's ever gotten from them. You'd be able to tell when a certain line of questioning is causing them to clam up, so you can back off, or rephrase the question in a less antagonistic way. This is just a small way that behavioral analysis can help you.

When you understand the remaining 93 percent of communication, there's a world of difference in every aspect of life. It could be the difference between moving forward in your career or remaining stuck in the muck. It's how you get ahead of the curve in your field. It's the reason your boss trusts you with more responsibility and promotes you – or doesn't.

Reading people correctly can save you a ton of heartbreak. Imagine a world where everyone figured out on the first date whether a relationship with the person sitting across from them was worth pursuing. See? No heartbreaks. All dates would end with a handshake, and "Let's do this again, never."

The ability to analyze people correctly and clearly means you can easily settle issues at home. You can keep the peace with your employees or colleagues at work. Don't go through unnecessary, rowdy, sometimes violent arguments, unless you're into that or some reason (in which case, you need to read a different book and see a mental health professional).

Reading people is a skill that anyone and everyone will reap benefits from. Salespeople and advertising companies know the value of grasping behavioral psychology. Don't be surprised that these companies will happily hire people with a degree in psychology because they expect them to figure out how to turn basic human behavior into profit.

The human mind and its workings are often being exploited for good or bad. You've been to a store. Have you ever asked yourself why you always make last-minute buys at the checkout counter? It's because things have been deliberately set up that way. Those items were put right in your line of vision, so as you're paying for the stuff you did plan to buy, you wind up thinking, "Meh, might as well get that pack of gum. The babe likes that."

Are You a Master People Reader?

Some people think that they are absolute pros at reading others. You've probably been in this situation: You're at a party, sipping on your drink, taking it all in, feeling at one with yourself and the universe at that moment. How blessed you are to know such awesome people! Suddenly, some random person walks up to you and asks, "Hey, what's with the long face?"

You tell them that you're fine, but they insist you can't be because you're looking so down. You offer the classic line, "This is my happy face," but they do not believe it. They've probably even pulled up a chair to sit by you so you can talk about your deep, dark problems. Well, if you weren't sad before, you're sad now. Maybe, you can relate to this experience. Maybe, you've even been guilty of this mistake yourself.

So, here's a quiz for you to figure out just how great you are at reading people on a basic level, with no crystal balls. Many of these feelings are often misinterpreted. You have four options for each question. Try to see how many you can accurately answer. Watch someone you know well. Analyze them. Then ask them how they are feeling. Did you get it right?

1. Fear. Embarrassment. Surprise. Anger.
2. Politeness. Interest. Happiness. Flirtatiousness.
3. Disgust. Sadness. Anger. Pain.
4. Amusement. Sadness. Shame. Embarrassment.
5. Contempt. Pride. Anger. Excitement.
6. Interest. Fear. Compassion. Surprise.
7. Contempt. Sadness. Disgust. Shame.
8. Anger. Disgust. Pain. Sadness.
9. Flirtatiousness. Embarrassment. Love. Desire.
10. Pain. Anger. Sadness. Shame.
11. Anger. Compassion. Interest. Sadness.
12. Desire. Excitement. Amusement. Surprise.
13. Interest. Happiness. Desire. Surprise.
14. Shame. Compassion. Sadness. Disgust.

15. Love. Desire. Disgust. Contempt.
16. Sadness. Shame. Embarrassment. Pride.
17. Compassion. Happiness. Desire. Politeness.
18. Love. Embarrassment. Shame. Sadness.
19. Sadness. Guilt. Disgust. Pain.
20. Satisfaction. Compassion. Love. Flirtatiousness.

Chapter Two: Understanding Human Behavior & Psychology

We all hold strong opinions about such things as whether the death penalty should remain, whether the church and state should mingle and whether there should be pineapple on pizza. These are attitudes we all have around certain issues. These attitudes can dictate what you believe and how you behave, as well. Let's talk about attitude some more.

The Psychologist's Definition of Attitude

Psychologists say attitude is the tendency to judge things, issues, people, and events in a light, whether good, bad, or uncertain. Attitude comprises three components:

> • The affective component, being how you feel about the person, thing, or issue in question.
> • The behavioral component, which is how your attitude affects your behavior.
> • The cognitive component, which involves your beliefs and thoughts on the matter.

These are the ABC's of attitude.

Attitude can also be looked at in terms of being explicit and implicit. Where implicit attitudes are just beneath the surface, unconscious, they still affect our patterns of belief and the way we behave. Explicit attitudes are those we know of, which obviously affect our thoughts and actions.

Your attitude can be because of experience, sociocultural norms, and learned behavior from, say, the classical conditioning that advertisers use on us to get us to think about things a certain way. You can also develop an attitude, thanks to operant conditioning, which involves getting feedback from your environment about your behavior. Your attitude could also result from simple observation of everyone around you, just like how, as a child, you observed your parents and likely took on their beliefs and behaviors in certain situations.

Most folks assume that attitude and behavior are often in line with each other, but that is not the case. For instance, an undercover DEA agent could have an attitude of disgust with drug dealers and illegal substances, but that doesn't mean they're going to immediately cuff everyone they know is a dealer. In the same way, you may strongly support a candidate, but you might not necessarily go out to vote.

Behavior Analysis

Behavior analysis is based on the tenets of behaviorism. There are three ways psychologists analyze behavior:

- Experimentally investigating behaviors.
- Applying learned facts about behavior to real-world contexts.
- Analyzing behavior based purely on concepts, theoretically, historically, philosophically, and methodologically.

Techniques for Behavior Analysis

To make things even more practical, here are the techniques used by the pros to analyze behavior:

1. **Prompting:** The behavior analyst will trigger the response they seek by using a prompt. This prompt could be a visual cue or a verbal cue.

2. **Chaining:** Here, the behavior analyst turns a task into chunks, smaller bits. The easiest of the tasks (or the first one) will be taught first. As soon as that task has been handled, then they can move on to the next, creating a chain that only ends when the sequence is complete.

3. **Shaping:** The behavior in focus is altered bit by bit. With each step the subject takes toward the preferred behavior, there is a reward.

Your Brain and Your Behavior

Biopsychology studies how your brain, it's neurotransmitters (or chemicals) and other parts of your body affect your thoughts, feelings, and behavior. This field is also called behavioral neuroscience.

The point of this study is to analyze the way the biological processes in your brain work with cognitions, emotions, and all other strictly mental processes in your brain.

There have been phenomenal discoveries about the way the brain functions based on biological factors. Your spinal cord and brain make up your central nervous system (CNS). Your cerebral cortex, the outer part of your brain, is what handles sensation, cognition, emotions, and motor skills.

Your brain has precisely four lobes:

• The frontal lobe handles high-level cognition, motor skills, and the expression of self through language.

- The occipital lobe helps you understand all information and stimuli visual in nature.

- The parietal lobe is the reason you can process all tactile stimuli, among other things. It's why you know when to get your hand off the hot stove or why that massage feels so good.

- The temporal lobe processes auditory information, helping you understand language and sound. It also helps you with processing your memories, among other things.

You also have a **peripheral nervous system** made up of:

- The sensory or afferent division, which takes all sensory info to your central nervous system for processing.

- The motor or efferent division works to connect your central nervous system to your glands and muscles.

Then there's your **autonomic nervous system** made up of:

- The sympathetic nervous system handles your fight, flight, or freeze reflex in response to danger and stress.

- The parasympathetic nervous system, which brings your body to a restful state and handles your digestive process, among other things.

Within this wonderful brain of yours are chemicals known as neurotransmitters. These take information from neuron to neuron, and for sending information from a brain to a body part, and vice versa. Examples of neurotransmitters are dopamine, which handles learning and movement. When you have too much of that, you're at risk for disorders like schizophrenia. Too little, and you might have to contend with Parkinson's disease.

Dopamine is a feel-good hormone. When you feel good, it's only natural to indulge in behavior that continues to perpetuate that good feeling. In this way, and in so many other ways, your brain affects your behavior. If the frontal lobe was unusual in any way, that would affect the way you think, which would affect your behavior.

Other Factors that Affect Human Behavior

People behave the way they do depend on several other factors besides the brain. Here are some:

- Abilities: These are the things you've learned from observing your environment and the things that you're naturally gifted at. There are three classes of abilities: Intellectual abilities are the sort that involves logic, intelligence, the ability to communicate and analyze. Physical abilities would be your strength, speed, stamina, motor skills, and body coordination. Self-awareness abilities involve the way you feel about the tasks you must do.

- Gender: Whether you're a man or a woman, you've got equal chances as the other to do well mentally, or at a specific job. However, society respects the difference between both. For instance, when a woman is usually the caregiver for kids, it's not unusual behavior for her to be absent from work sometimes.

- Race and Culture: it's not proper to ascribe behavior based on culture and race, but it happens, and this can influence behavior. You may be of a certain race, which has had to deal with certain stereotypes. You're deliberate about behaving differently.

- Perception: Perception is how you turn data from your senses into useful information you can work with. There are six types of perception: The perception of sound, touch, taste, speech, other senses, and the social world.

- Genetics: Your genetic makeup can also influence your behavior. This is because your genes have done an excellent job of preserving the responses your ancestors had to certain situations. For instance, a child's genetic makeup might dictate whether they walk at three months, or eight months. This genetic influence on behavior has larger implications, but thankfully, you don't have to worry. Your behavior can change for the better and is not necessarily set in genes, or stone.

- Environment: The environment plays a huge role in behavior. Take a pair of twins at birth and separate them, one in India and the other in Sweden. They probably would be as different as sky and ground. The cultures in these two places are different, and so behavior would naturally be different to some extent.

The Three Laws of Human Behavior

Law #1: Behavior will often align with the status quo, unless there's a reward or a risk that necessitates change. If you've done something repeatedly, so it becomes a habit that becomes the status quo for you. Think of it like inertia, according to Newton's first law of motion. If your behavior changes, then something must force it to, whether it's a bad thing (like an inability to breathe well if you're a smoker) or a good thing (like a bump in pay raise when you actually give your work your all).

Law #2: Your behavior boils down to your kind of person and your environment. You didn't just drop down to the earth with an already formed set of behaviors. You can thank Kurt Lewin for boiling down behavior to your state or traits, and your environment. These elements are interdependent in that you can't predict behavior based only on your understanding of who someone is, how they think, and feel, nor can you predict behavior based on the environment they're in. You need a combo of both.

Law #3: Every decision you make will have trade-offs and can lead to unplanned consequences. That's just the fact of life. You want to start working out. The pro: you get fit and healthy. The con: you've got to make time for it, maybe go shopping for new gym clothes too. It's all about opportunity cost, or, "What am I sacrificing if I choose to do this thing." There are also consequences you don't intend to have or don't anticipate. For instance, you could decide to workout with some loud music to feel pumped and motivated, but your neighbors might be trying to get some sleep after a long night shift and might not appreciate the noise. That's known as the tragedy of commons.

Techniques Used by Behavioral Psychologists

Here are techniques that behavioral psychologists use which you can implement in your life now:

1. Detangling Cognitive Distortions: You can detangle the errors in thinking you have by yourself, but you must first know the ones you suffer from the most. Here's a quick run-through of possible distortions you might be dealing with:

a) Black-and-white or polarized thinking: You think everything is this or that, and there are no shades of gray, no in-betweens.

b) Filtering: You focus only on the negative aspects of things, instead of the positives and negatives, or vice versa.

c) Jumping to conclusions: You are certain of things with no evidence.

d) Overgeneralization: You take one thing that happened one time with one sort of person and assume that is the law with every other person who looks or sounds like that. Or you assume you failed at a new business, so you'll fail at others.

e) Personalization: You think everything you say or do affects others, even when that's actually an exaggeration. For instance, you assume being late to a party would throw it off schedule.

f) Minimizing or Magnifying/Catastrophizing: You assume that the worst will happen if it hasn't already, all because of an event that's not as terrible as you thought. Or, you assume positive things are not that important, like when you do a stellar job, or you're a great friend.

g) Fairness fallacy: You take the need for everything and everyone to be fair to the extreme, and this makes you unhappy.

h) Control fallacy: You feel like all things that happen either are entirely on you or entirely because of forces beyond your control. You don't allow yourself to think that it could be both not one or the other.

i) *Shoulds*: These are the assumptions and rules you have about how you and others *should* act. When these rules are not followed, you get mad.

j) Blaming: When things don't line up as you expected, you allocate responsibility to someone else or something else besides yourself. Maybe you blame others for the way you act or feel.

k) Change Fallacy: You think people should change to suit your mood. You assume your happiness lies in the way others behave, so if they don't change as you'd like them to, you get upset.

l) Emotional logic: You feel a certain way, so you assume the way you feel must be true. However, emotions are not the best go-to when you want objective truth.

m) The fallacy of "Heaven's Reward": You think that when you deny yourself good things and sacrifice yourself, you'll get a great reward for your selfless deeds. However, when those rewards don't come, you feel bitter.

n) Always being in the right: You find it hard to accept that you could be wrong. It matters deeply that you're always right. Your rightness matters so much that other people's feelings could burn to ashes for all you care. You have trouble accepting you're wrong.

o) Mislabeling or global labeling: This is a generalization to the extreme. You take one or two events or traits, and you project that and make it a universal thing. You failed at riding a bike, so you believe you will fail at swimming and life. There's also assuming just because someone says something you think is critical or rude, that they're anything but friendly. Often you use overly exaggerated ways to describe that one act they did. Your roommate didn't do the dishes last night? By Jove, what a filthy rat!

2. Cognitive restructuring: This involves looking at how you got these distortions, and why you buy into them. When you discover the beliefs that power them, you can challenge and change them.

3. Journaling: As you journal, you assess your thoughts and moods, and your reactions. There's no better way to get to know yourself, your patterns of thoughts, your emotional leanings, and how to cope with, adapt to, or change them.

4. Nightmare exposure and re-scripting: Dealing with nightmares? Then you can use this technique. You bring your nightmare to mind and let it drum up the emotions you felt. Once you feel the discomfort and fear, you can figure out what you'd rather feel and then create a new image that works with your preferred emotion to replace the nightmare.

5. Interoceptive exposure: This is great for dealing with anxiety and panic. You expose yourself to the bodily sensations you're afraid of, so you can get the usual response. As you do, the toxic beliefs with the sensations arise, and you hold on to the sensation without seeking to avoid them, or distract yourself, so you can learn new things about it. It shows you that your panic symptoms are not life-threatening. Uncomfortable, but not dangerous.

6. Progressive muscle relaxation: Lie in a comfortable position, and then scan your body by muscle group, starting from your toes, to your head. Breathing deeply, you tense each muscle group, and then relax it several times before moving upwards. You can check out YouTube videos for guided relaxation sessions.

7. Exposure and response prevention: If you suffer from obsessive-compulsive disorder, this can help. Expose yourself to the things that trigger your compulsion and do your best to refrain from your usual response. Do this repeatedly. Journal your feelings as you do, and notice as your compulsions weaken.

8. Relaxed breathing: This is a great mindfulness technique. There are so many ways to use this, from guided meditations to unguided ones. Simply bring your attention to your breath. Breathe in deeply through your nose, and then exhale through your lips, slightly parted. Your exhale will be longer than the inhale. That's okay. This helps with OCD, depression, panic disorder, anxiety, and a host of other illnesses.

9. Relive the scene until the end: This works if you're battling anxiety and fear. It's basically an experiment where you imagine the worst possible scenario of how things could go. It helps you realize that even in the worst case, you will still manage simply fine.

Chapter Three: The 16 Personality Types

Now, let's talk about personality. What is it, really? Personality refers to the differences that exist from one person to another, in terms of their set patterns of thought, emotion, and behavior. Studying personality involves considering the differences that exist in certain personality traits, like being generally irritable or sociable. It's also about understanding how all the various aspects of a person come together to form a complete being.

The Myers-Briggs Personality Types

There are 16 personality types according to the Myers-Briggs classification of personalities. Let's sink our teeth into each one, a la Dracula.

The Architect

This personality is an imaginative and strategic thinker with a plan for just about everything. They are classified as Introverted, Intuitive, Thinking, Judging (INTJ). They are particular about details and have a great way of blending the rational with creativity. You'll find an Architect is a private person, with a rich, complex world within. This personality type is rare and capable of taking on more responsibility than most. The female Architect is almost a unicorn, difficult to find. It's tough for the Architect to find those that can deal with their constant analysis of everything. However, the Architect is not bogged down by analysis. They make swift decisions and are curious, yet focused, and ambitious. You won't find them wasting energy on trivial pursuits like gossip. The Architect is an interesting combination of a dreamer always looking on the bright side and a bitter pessimist. They're very innovative, thanks to their profound insights and logical thinking. They're a perfectionist in all they do. If you can't keep up with them, they will leave you far behind. Do you have rules? Your rules can go hug a powerline. They are not big on social skills. They won't shoot the breeze with you. They love to be out of the spotlight, but this doesn't mean they lack confidence.

The Logician

The Logician is Introverted, INtuitive, Thinking, and Prospecting (INTP). They think on their feet. If you need an unconventional way of looking at things or doing things, you can't go wrong with them. They're almost as rare as the Architect — and that's actually a great thing. The last thing the Logician wants is to be "common." They love that they're the inventive, creative ones, with no-box thinking and an impressive intellect. The logician sees the pattern in everything. They are also quick to see where something doesn't add up, so please don't lie to them. The funny thing about the Logician and lies is that you must be wary of what they say. No, they're not liars, but they open their minds up to you while still working on ideas that still need a lot of working out. Think of yourself as a sounding board to them. Don't take it personally. The Logician may not deliver when they said they would, but they do deliver. They might seem lost in their dreams, but really, they're always thinking. From the second they realize they're awake, ideas flood their minds in torrents. This makes them seem a tad detached, but it's nothing to worry about. They're pretty chill to be around, especially when they're with people who have the same interests, or close and trusted friends. However, the Logician doesn't do well with new people, as they're suddenly shy. Banter can turn to battle if they suspect you're critical of their ideas.

The Inspector

The Inspector is Introverted, Sensing, Thinking, Judging (ISTJ). They can seem a tad intimidating when you're in the room with them, especially when you have no connection or relationship to them. They seem rather proper, serious, and all about formalities. They value all things traditional and old-school. They love the time-honored values of hard work, patience, honor, and responsibility in their society and culture. They are calm, upright, reserved, and thoughtful. Unfortunately, they are often misunderstood.

The Counselor

The counselor is Introverted, Intuitive, Feeling, Judging (INFJ). They have the most brilliant minds and are highly creative. The way they think about things is unusual, and unfortunately, their viewpoint is often misunderstood. The INFJ is about depth with thought and speech. There's got to be substance to whatever currently holds their attention. They're not the kind to be content with the superficial or buy into the shiny bright tinsel you're coating your words with. They are always scanning for much better ways to deal with challenging issues. Some people might think this odd, but that's just the INFJ's ways.

The Giver

Meet the ENFJ: Extroverted, Intuitive, Feeling, Judging. They're the giving type. They're very charismatic and have grand ideas. They're the outspoken person in the room who is bound by ethics and principles. This means that the ENFJ finds it easy to relate with people from all walks of life and all other personality types. They depend on their feelings and intuition much more than the real world. This fondness for their imagination can be problematic for them, and those who deal with them. They're not about living in the now, as they'd rather lose themselves in abstract thoughts about what is possible in the future.

The Craftsman

This is the Intuitive, Sensing, Thinking, Perceiving (ISTP) personality. They have an air of mystery to them that is never unraveled, leaving them misunderstood. While they are all about logical and rational thought, they can quite demonstrate enthusiasm and spontaneity. It's not easy to gauge their personality traits, compared to the other types of personalities. You can't beat yourself up for this, though. Even those who are close to the ISTP can't say with certainty what they will do next. The Craftsman is spontaneous, but they're also crafty at hiding that spontaneity from you and I, preferring to show up as responsible and logical.

The Provider

This Extroverted, Sensing, Feeling, and Judging (ESFJ) personality can't help but be social. They have an innate desire to connect with others socially. They love nothing more than to make others happy, and they're the darlings of the lot. The ESFJ is usually the star of the show, and they always show up for family and friends, whether that means personal needs or setting up social events for everyone to get together. The Provider is loved by most, and it's easy to see why.

The Idealist

Introverted, Intuitive, Feeling, and Perceiving (INFP). These introverts, like other introverts, are reserved and quiet. No, this differs from being shy. The Idealist would rather not make themselves the subject of discussion, especially not when you're just meeting for the first time. You'll find them on their own, in quiet places, which lets them figure out the world they live in. The INFP is a huge fan of symbols and signs, always digging into them to find the actual meaning of their life. It's not hard for the INFP to get lost in their heads. They are The Idealist. This can be a good thing when they put their thoughts to practical use or a bad thing when they wind up drowning in a sea of ideas, fantasies, and other thoughts.

The Performer

Extroverted, Sensing, Feeling, Perceiving (ESFP) - the Performer is just that: An entertainer. They're great at distracting and amusing the rest of us, and they just love to be in the limelight. They're often the one in the middle of a circle of laughing people, recounting tales in the most interesting ways. They are rather thoughtful and incredibly open to exploring the world. They're passionate about learning, and about sharing what they've learned with others. The Performer loves to have company. They're great at social and interpersonal skills. The life of the party, it's never a dull moment with them — and far be it from them to turn down a chance to have all eyes on them. Don't let this put you off, though. The Performer is a warm person. You'll find them quite friendly and generous. Also, if you want a sympathetic ear, then they'll give you both of theirs. This personality cares about how everyone is doing.

The Champion

Extroverted, Intuitive, Feeling, and Perceiving, the ENFP is an individual to the core. They don't follow. They don't fall in line, and they don't give a rip about the status quo. They're the ones who love to rock the boat. They'll find their own way of doing things. They'll find a creative way to wear a boring tie. Their ideas, habits, and actions are anything but regular. The Champion is not fond of people who only color within the lines. Try to make them follow set rules, and they'd be miserable. However, the Champion does enjoy being with the right people, and nothing is more pleasurable than connecting on an intuitive level with others. The ENFP is usually "all in their feels" in the way they do things. It's not a bad thing, actually, since they are thoughtful in their words and actions, and are able to perceive subtext and cues.

The Doer

The Doer is Extroverted, Sensing, Thinking, and Perceiving. They're the reason for the term "social butterfly." They enjoy interacting with people and are energized by emotions and feelings.

Now, don't be quick to assume this means the Doer is flippant about life. Far from it. They love reasoning, using logic to arrive at conclusions that make sense — as long as it doesn't keep them from letting their thoughts roam wild and doing what they set out to do. To hold the ESTP's attention, you'd better have more than just abstract ideas and theories for them. They want to go, and they want to go now! They want to act. They're the sort likely to make a move and deal with the consequences as they come up. For them, this is much better than just sitting on their hands or thinking of contingency plans.

The Supervisor

The ESTJ — Extroverted, Sensing, Thinking, Judging - is about traditional values. They love dedication. They treasure truth, honor, and being organized. The Supervisor has an extraordinarily strong moral compass. They will act only if it's right to do so, and whatever they do must be socially acceptable. It's not easy to clearly state the right and the wrong way to do things, but the Supervisor will surely step in to lead the way for everyone else, letting their personal thoughts be known. The Supervisor is the model citizen; the one everyone goes to when they need sound advice. This personality is more than happy to give you the counsel you need.

The Commander

The Commander is an ENTJ — Extroverted, intuitive, Thinking, Judging. They're about dealing with all things around them using discipline and logic. When they've satisfied their need for logic and discipline, then they can allow their intuition to step in. The Commander is a born leader. Of all the personality types, the Commander has leadership in their blood. They're okay with taking charge. Scratch that, they relish the chance to be in charge. The Commander believes in possibilities, so they aren't floored by challenges that come their way. The Commander welcomes problems, seeing them as an opportunity to do and be better. They are unafraid of making the hard decisions, to which they always give a lot of thought. The Commander does not wait for life to happen.

They go out there and create opportunities where there seems to be none.

The Nurturer

Intuitive, Sensing, Feeling, Judging, the Nurturer will always be generous. They're the philanthropist, you know, always willing and happy to give back. If you were ever kind to them, then they will return that kindness to you seventy times seven. That's just the way they are. If you're fortunate enough to have the Nurturer believe in you, then trust they will go out for you with no hidden agenda. The Nurturer also upholds the ideals they believe in with that same unbridled passion. They're the kindest, warmest personalities you will ever have the pleasure of knowing. Sensitive to the way others feel, the Nurturer will always hold peace, cooperation, and harmony in high esteem. They're always considerate of others, and very aware of how people around them feel. Also, they can't help but bring out the best in everyone they meet.

The Visionary

This Extroverted, Intuitive, Thinking, Perceiving (ENTP) personality is also rare. They are extroverts, but they don't do well with small talk. Not even a little bit. Because of this, they don't do well at parties or social scenes, particularly when everyone around them is of a quite different personality type than they are. The Visionary is deeply knowledgeable about things. Their intelligence is unparalleled. These two traits make it, so they need constant mental stimulation, so they don't get bored. They love a chance to talk facts and theories, diving into every little detail, making sure you get it right. The Visionary is rational, logical, and objective in how they deal with everything. They approach arguments the same way, so if you ever find yourself in a verbal fencing match with them, know that they expect you to be logical and rational.

The Composer

Say hello to the Intuitive, Sensing, Feeling, Perceiving personality. The funny thing about these introverts is that they don't always seem introverted. Sure, they have some stumbling and fumbling going on when they try to connect with you for the first time, but give them enough time to warm up, and they become very friendly, warm, and approachable. The ISFP is a fun person to hang out with. They can act on a whim, the spontaneous Composer. You'd have a great tie going to various events with them, whether planned or unplanned. The Composer has one intention: Make the most of life. They are all about being present, and this helps others see the wonder of the ordinary moments they take for granted. The Composer seeks new discoveries and adventures. They value understanding others, as they'll often get great golden nuggets of wisdom from each encounter. So, while they may be introverted, they actually love meeting new people more than the other introvert personalities do.

Tips for Identifying Each Type

1. ISFJs, ESFJs, ISTJs, and ESTJs talk about past stories and experiences. They are practical and often down to earth. They love to hark back to tradition and draw on their personal experiences. They remember what has worked well, and they use that info when it's needed. They love routine and find security in it. These types are loyal, responsible, and dedicated. They love supporting their communities and families.

2. The ESTPs, ISTPs, ESFPs, and ISFPs are great at taking in all the details going on in the now. They are very well aware of their environment and know how to make the present count. They are adventurous, up for a good time, easy-going, and flexible. You will notice that they know how to disentangle themselves gracefully through the obstacles that present themselves physically. They have great spatial awareness and love to engage with the world outside of them, using a hands-on approach. They love to interact with ideas and will take opportunities to act on them.

3. The INFJs, ENFJs, INTJs, and ENTJs are mostly future-oriented. They see the big picture and figure out the possible ways

that things will work out by paying attention to clues, patterns, and connections that most people miss. They are drawn to the unknown, the mystical, the existential, and theoretical. They are very single-minded people, with extreme focus and clear-cut plans for the way they want life to go. They often will get an instinctual nudge about how things will work out, or about what steps to take next. Often, these hunches turn out for the good, even though they seem to come out of nowhere. These types are very intense, so don't let that scare you off.

4. The ISTPs, ESTPs, INTPs, and ENTPs are all about logic. You can tell who they are because they love to learn for the fun of it, not to impress people. They don't want your admiration; they don't care about following rules. These personalities will use language that indicates they create their own destiny as they want to.

5. The ENTJs, INTJs, ESTJs, and ISTJs, are very productive. It's hard to miss their confidence. They plan ahead, and they're all about making things happen in the most efficient way. They want to put their stuff out there. You'll notice they're the ones who don't procrastinate but prefer to get things over and done with way ahead of time.

6. The INFPs, ENFPs, ISFPs, and ESFPs are a unique, authentic lot who care about the values they hold. "To thy own self be true" is their motto if you observe them closely. They're about making an impact for the causes that matter to them. Their morals have nothing to do with where they are, or what society says. They are averse to any fake vibes. Also, they're open-minded, very empathetic, and the best listeners you could ever hope to have. They aren't so quick to share their feelings with people they haven't gotten to know yet.

7. The ISFJs, ESFJs, ENFJs, and INFJs are friendly and full of empathy. They can easily tell what your mood or emotions are. They do their best to maintain upbeat morale wherever they go, with everyone they deal with. No matter who they're talking to, they

know how to weave their words in such a way it lands right and has a great impact. For them, it's about values, harmony, and ethics.

Chapter Four: The Secrets of Speed Reading

Speed reading is about figuring out someone's temperament or personality type. You can quickly figure out the sort of person you're dealing with by asking them certain questions. The Myers-Briggs classification of personalities gives you 16 personalities, but they're all in four major classes, so don't be overwhelmed with trying to remember them all. Learn to speed read because it will help you relate better with people.

Breaking Down the Categories of Myers' Briggs

Extrovert/Introvert. This is about what energizes you the most. Do you draw your energy from being with other people? Then you are most definitely an extrovert. If you don't get your energy from being with people, but from being alone, then you're an introvert. Most people erroneously assume that introversion and extroversion are about being outgoing or not. That's not it at all. There are extremely outgoing introverts who are very expressive, believe it or not. Introversion and extroversion come down to your *source of energy.*

Sensory/Intuition. What this category covers is how you absorb information. Do you absorb it internally, allowing your ideas and thoughts to percolate and bubble up from within? Or are you the sort who pays more attention to your five senses? If you're a "thought percolator," then you're intuitive. However, if you primarily get your information from the environment you're in, wherever that is, then you're sensory or "sensing."

Thinking/Feeling. What this comes down to is how you process the information you get. Are you the person who chews on facts, figures, and concrete data before anything else? If this comes naturally to you, then you're definitely "Thinking." However, if you usually first process stuff like emotion, the impact a certain action or event would have on others, values, and things of that nature, then you are "Feeling. "

Judging/Perceiving. This is about how you decide in your day to day life. If you're Judging, you decide faster and earlier. You're very structured, and you love order. You make well-informed decisions way before they're due, and you would much rather decide way before the deadline, and not at the last minute. This way, you can hold on to your structure and the sense of order in your life. The Sensory Judging, in particular, is crazy about lists, as they help them stay organized. If you perceive, on the other hand, then you're a lot more flexible than the Judging. You're so flexible that you tend to wait until the very last minute to decide on something. You do this because you're still acquiring and processing information and resources and getting to know the options available to you.

The reason for this is simple. You want to make sure that you make the most of the time that you've got between the present and the looming deadline to choose the best course of action. You're always about looking for a better solution or fix than what is currently available.

As for the Judging, you are a heavy procrastinator. However, that's not accurate. What's really going on is you need to find the best options because that really matters to you. And, often, you do wind up finding said better options anyway.

Waiting till the last minute does not leave you stressed. The Judging personality would be stressed, having to wait as you do. You, on the other hand, would be stressed out trying to decide early or plan and make lists and get organized. Others would say you perform well under pressure. You probably have the most brilliant ideas when the deadline looms closer.

The thing about these four categories of personalities is that they are not black-and-white. They are preferences or your automatic behavioral response to events in life. It's not like you're strictly an introvert or an extrovert, or strictly a judger or a perceiver.

Think of them as your initial preference, or what you're most naturally inclined to act like. For instance, some extroverts can be fine with being on their own. Some of them voluntarily want to be alone. Go figure. You have two hands. You have the option of using either, but only one hand will be dominant unless you're ambidextrous.

Another thing to note about these categories is that they have scores or grades to them, from zero to thirty. To keep things simple, think of it more like a range from a slight preference to a strong preference. People have their preferences, but they can think through all these categories, and as they mature, they think through the weaker aspects or slight preferences, giving them strength.

Speed Reading People

Extrovert or Introvert?

Say you asked someone this question: When you're tired after a long day and need to unwind, do you prefer to head out to a party at the club, or would you rather go home and be alone?

Assume they answered, saying, "Yeah, I'd rather just go to a coffee shop and be alone." That's a curious answer that's very telling. Say you were to probe further, asking why a coffee shop. They might say, "Well, I like the sounds of other people in the background, but that's it. I actually just want to be by myself while I can hear others." Is this person an introvert or an extrovert? They're extroverted.

Here's another question you could ask when speed reading someone: How often do you like to spend time by yourself? They might say, maybe 20 percent of the time.

Then you can follow that up with this question: When you're alone, how long do you like to spend by yourself until you decide you need company? Even among just extroverts, you would get a variety of answers. Some want to be alone a whole day. Some want to be alone for just 30 minutes. See? Nothing is black and white here. These questions will let you know whether they're extroverts or introverts.

Sensory or Intuitive?

To figure out where someone lies in this category, ask this: When you're learning about your world, do you spend more of your time paying attention to the stuff you can see, touch, and smell, or do you just have ideas that start to well up in your mind and you no longer follow what's happening around you? What describes you best?

Another good question to ask: Do you find it frustrating and downright confusing when you have to deal with way too much theory?

Here's another question: Are you better at coming up with original ideas, or would you rather implement them?

If you're dealing with a sensory person, then you've got to communicate with them in concrete terms. If you're dealing with intuitive, they love to have fun with ideas, but they're great at taking an abstract idea and making it concrete — unless they're on the extreme end of the spectrum of intuitiveness, in which case nothing might ever get done if they don't have the *Sensory* around.

Thinking or Feeling?

Here is a question you can ask to figure out which end of the thinking or feeling spectrum the other person is at:

When you're learning something new, do you think about the facts, figures, and other details involved, or do you first wonder how this information will affect other people and their emotions and values?

Both the Thinking and Feeling are important in society. Thinking might get lost in their wonderful world of details but forget about the human element. This is where the Feeling comes into balance the equation, especially in such industries that involve caregiving.

Judging or Perceiving?

To figure out which category someone prefers, simply ask them, Would you rather make lists and plan ahead, or do you prefer to keep things loose and surprise yourself?

Are you stressed out by waiting till the last minute to do things?

The J and the P are valuable in society, whether at work or at home. A great way to maintain balance is to make sure there are always plans and those plans are executed, and then that there's room for optimization. This way, the Judging can get their planning done and feel at ease knowing they've covered all bases, while the Perceiving can get involved in the optimization process where they can see new angles or ways of doing things.

If you understand the way the core of the Myers-Briggs personalities, or any other classification of personalities, work then you should have no problem crafting the right questions to figure out where people stand.

The ability to speed read people is essential. This is how you can make sure there's peace at home and that at work, things are running as they should. It's a great way to build the right sort of friendships and partnerships because you can cut through all the clutter and connect with them on a genuine level.

Common Mistakes When Reading People

Reading people isn't just about asking those questions, although those are helpful. It's also about studying body language. However, not everyone gets that right. Here are common mistakes:

- Not paying attention to the context. Maybe their lips are pressed together only because they're dry. Maybe they have their arms wrapped around their chest because it's cold. Notice the context before you decide how someone is feeling or what they're thinking.

- Not looking out for clusters. You can't just say someone is lying because they looked up and to the left or whatever. Life is not a poker game. Often, a combination of actions let you know what's going on with someone. Look at these behaviors in clusters, not singles.

- Not figuring out the baseline behavior. If someone blinks a lot when they speak, naturally, but they're suddenly not blinking, that should tell you something is off. Maybe they're lying, or they're holding back, or they're afraid, or they're excited, or something. If you're not sure what it is, then you should see error number one. Pay attention to context.

- Not being aware of your biases. When you don't like someone, it will make you judge them unfairly. Also, when people compliment you, it will affect the way you see them, even if it's on an unconscious level. You must be very neutral when you're attempting to read someone because some people will attempt to make you see them in a different light than they truly are. Whether that is intentional is another matter up for debate.

Chapter Five: How to Read Body Language

Communication doesn't just happen with words. It's in the stuff you don't say. If you will have fulfilling relationships in your personal and professional life, then you've got to learn to communicate. What this means is it's not enough to speak the same language. You've got to pay attention to such things as tone, facial expression, and body language. You've got to pay attention to nonverbal communication.

Why does nonverbal communication matter so much? Because often, body language is the most accurate depiction of what's going on in a person's mind. It's all about various expressions, mannerisms, and other forms of physical behavior that take the words being spoken and wrap them up in a rich tapestry of meaning.

We all know nonverbal communication, some more than others, of course. You could converse with someone and feel something's off about them. You probably were picking up on nonverbal cues, like eye contact, vocal tone, hand gestures, body posture, and so on. Knowing how your body talks is a useful skill because you can detect who's genuine and who's not. You can also communicate so it fosters trust, openness, mutual respect, and bonding. Even when you're silent, you'll know how to be. Trust me when I say even in your silence, your body speaks loudly.

When the words you speak and your body language do not match each other, there is a lack of congruence between the two, and you can seem dishonest. In such situations, people will often go with what they noticed, not what you said, since there's no truer language than your body's.

Why Nonverbal Communication Matters

To know the relevance of nonverbal communication, consider the roles it plays. First, when you're honest, it helps to strengthen whatever message it is you're passing across verbally.

When someone's lying, body language can be immensely helpful. Often, it will contradict the words coming out of their mouth, so you know to take them with a pinch of salt.

When you don't feel like talking, or you're where speaking would not be ideal, body language can save the day. Your expression and the posture you've adopted can help folks figure out what's going on with you, sometimes even better than words could.

Nonverbal communication acts as a wonderful complement to whatever you're saying. For instance, if your colleague were to say, "Hey, great job on that presentation!" You'd love that, naturally. But, if they said that, and gave you a literal pat on the back, that would make you feel even better, as it communicates even stronger the sincerity of their compliment and adoration for you. That's how awesome nonverbal communication is. It can strengthen or underscore the message you're passing across.

Forms of Nonverbal Communication

Posture and body movement can communicate a lot about you at first glance. Posture isn't necessarily about whether you always walk with your head held high and shoulders back because you went to some finishing school. It's more about the carriage. The way you hold your head, sit, walk, and stand. It's the way you move and all the subtle movements you make, which are very telling about you.

Facial expressions are another form of verbal communication – often more expressive than body language since you can communicate quite a range of emotions and messages with your face alone. The great thing about facial expressions is that they're universal, remaining the same no matter the culture.

Eye contact is another key form of nonverbal communication. Sustained eye contact, too little eye contact, or constantly broken eye contact all say various things. Your eyes can show disdain, interest, love, hate, affection, confusion, determination, and so much more. Eye contact is also a great way to determine whether you want to keep engaging someone in conversation or set them free already.

Gestures are unavoidable in everyday life. We point, wave, make the "hang loose" sign, flip someone the bird, slice the air with our hands, and all without thinking too much about it. Some gestures are the same all over the world. Some aren't. I'd be wary of making the OK sign in Brazil, Russia, Germany. Please don't do it.

Space is an interesting form of nonverbal communication. Some people have no concept of personal space. Sometimes, that's a cultural thing. Other times it's simply an inability to read the room. You may have had an experience in which someone was a little too far into in your space, and you felt extremely uncomfortable. Or amazingly comfortable, depending on who they are. With space, you can communicate intimacy, dominance, aggression, or affection.

Touch is another potent nonverbal communication. Think about that clammy, limp hand you once shook. Think about the other hand you shook – the firm, warm one. See how both handshakes most likely affected your perception of the other person? Touch communicates whether it's a stroke on the cheek, a hug, a grip on the arm, or an annoying pat on the head.

Voice is key in communication. It's not just about the words, but the way the words flow from you. You can read people's voices and get more meaning from them than what they're saying. The timing of their speech, pacing, volume, inflection, and tone can say a lot about what the other person is feeling.

Reading Body Language

When you're chatting with someone or addressing a group, here are things to look out for to let you know that the other party is at ease and interested in the conversation:

1. Eye contact is key. Too much can be bad as too little. You want just enough eye contact. If they engage with you visually for many seconds each time, then you have an interested audience. When someone is lying to you, they will often avoid holding your gaze. However, if someone makes a habit of lying, they will deliberately hold your gaze for longer to fix that problem. So, if you notice that someone is holding your gaze too long and too intensely, then they're probably not being honest. Another thing about prolonged eye contact is that it could be threatening, so remember that.

2. Body posture will let you know if they're interested or not. When they stand or sit in an erect position, and they take up a lot of physical space with their body, it means authority and power. It means they're very vested in the conversation. When speaking with someone, if you notice they've crossed their legs or their arms, they might not actually be interested in what you have to say. Be mindful of context, though. Maybe it's cold, so they've crossed their arms. Maybe they always look like they stepped out of a GQ magazine and naturally cross their legs like they're posing for a photo.

3. Genuine smiles are a plus. It's easy to fake a smile, so it seems like all is well, but you can tell when they're forcing it. With a real smile, the eyes crinkle at the corner, showing a pattern that looks

like a crow's feet (it's literally called "crow's feet"). This is how you know they do love talking with you.

4. The firmness of a handshake lets you know if this person wants to engage. If it's a firm grip, they're confident and poised. If it's weak, they may be nervous, or they may be secretly contemptuous, or uninterested. Remember that a very firm handshake could be a subtle sign of aggression.

5. Physical closeness will let you know how comfortable the other person is with you around. If they stand or sit close, then you know they're okay with being there. If they keep their distance, they either don't want to be there because they have something to do, or because they find being with you uncomfortable. This distance between people communicating with each other is known as proxemics, thanks to Edward T. Hall, an anthropologist. He says there are four levels of social distance: 6 to 8 inches shows a close, comfortable relationship, where both parties can hug, touch, whisper, and share any intimate actions. This is an intimate distance. 1.5 to 4 feet is the personal distance, where there are family members or good friends. Social distance is 4 to 12 feet, and this is the space acquaintances or coworkers will often have between each other. Public distance is 12 to 25 feet. This is the space you get between a speaker and their audience at a public speaking event.

6. Too much nodding is not good. They either want you to shut up already so they can get their two cents in, or they don't feel confident being with you. They might be nervous about what you think of them.

7. Are their brows furrowed? If they've got wrinkles in their forehead, and their eyebrows are trying to meet each other, then it means they're either feeling uneasy, or they're confused.

8. Fidgeting means that they're likely nervous, disinterested, or bored. It's when they make a lot of small, unnecessary hand movements, move around in their seat, keep touching their clothes or hair, or other things nearby. Be mindful of context again, as

some people like to fidget with things while they think. It might not necessarily mean they're nervous or bored.

More Tips for Reading Nonverbal Communication

Blinking is a natural thing. Some people blink more than others, however, there is still much to learn from nonverbal cue. When people blink too fast, they're probably uncomfortable or in distress. When someone barely blinks, then that's probably a sign they're doing their best to control their eye movements.

Pupil size is an admittedly subtle way to read someone, but still valid. Remember that light in the room can affect the size of the pupils. With that out of the way, it's possible for emotions to cause little changes in pupil size. Say someone's attracted to you. Chances are they're giving you "bedroom eyes," in that their pupils dilate.

The mouth speaks in more ways than one. Besides the words, you can tell a lot from a person's mouth. Are they biting or chewing their bottom lip? Then they may feel insecure, worried, or afraid. If they're biting said bottom lip while giving you a meaningful, flirty look as they hold your eyes, well, there's no worry or fear in what they're communicating. When they cover their mouth, they're probably covering a yawn or a cough, or maybe they're trying to disguise their disapproval.

If they're smiling, then there are lots of things that could be going on, from genuine joy to false happiness, cynicism, and sarcasm. Notice their lips: Are they pursed? Then they might be disapproving of you, find you, or what you're saying distasteful, or they may be disapproving. If their lips are turned up, then they're feeling happy. If they're turned down, they may be sad, or they may not approve. It could also be a pure grimace.

Gestures like a clenched fist could either be a show of solidarity or anger. A thumbs-up signal means approval, while the thumbs down mean disapproval. The V sign, where your middle and index finger are lifted and separated, means victory or peace. If you're in Australia or the UK, it's offensive. The OK gesture, where your thumb and index finger touch to form a circle while the other three fingers are extended, means "alright" or "okay." There are parts of Europe where it means, "you are nothing." If you use it in South American countries, then it carries a vulgar meaning.

Legs and arms matter. Crossed arms mean they're feeling defensive. Crossed legs away from you mean they don't like you, or they're not comfortable with you. Spread arms that take up more room is confident, as they're unconsciously making themselves seem larger, and by extension, more commanding. On the flip side, arms tucked close to their body is a way to keep attention off themselves or an indication they feel small or threatened. Standing with both hands on the hips could be a sign they feel aggressive, or that they're in control. Hands clasped behind the back could mean anger, boredom, or anxiety. Fidgeting or fingers that tap rapidly could mean frustration, boredom, or impatience. Crossed legs could mean they would like some privacy, or they are closed off from you.

Sitting up straight means they are paying attention. If they're hunched forwards, then they're either indifferent or bored. A closed posture where they hide their trunk, cross arms and legs, could mean they're not feeling friendly, or they're hostile, or anxious. When they have an open posture, they keep the body's trunk exposed, showing they are open, eager, willing, and friendly.

Chapter Six: How to Analyze Handwriting

Just like your body talks, so does your handwriting. Big whoop, right? It's just words on paper. No, it's a lot more than the words you write down. Your handwriting can be a dead giveaway of how you felt in the moment you were writing it, or how you are in general. It can offer a baseline for figuring out your personality, feelings, character, and intentions. The science of analyzing handwriting is known as graphology.

Things to Keep in Mind about Graphology

1. Take it with a pinch of salt. Don't assume someone is a crook just because they've got crooked writing. Graphologists say they can find your personality in your handwriting. This is true, but only to a certain extent. You need to also recall you're not an actual expert on graphology, and there are a lot of other things going on with handwriting which graphologists consider before passing judgment on people based on their writing. Please don't judge people based on their handwriting alone. If you do, stay away from doctors, since they are legendary with their illegible handwriting. See? Doesn't make any sense.

2. You will need a proper writing sample. This would ideally be some cursive writing on unlined paper. Remember, though, that not everyone learned to write cursive, so don't assume they're a psycho for writing straight with no frills. If you want to analyze someone's handwriting, you will need more than one sample. Get a few, making sure each was written hours apart. The thing about handwriting is that it changes depending on the mood and circumstance. Having several samples will help you get a baseline for what their handwriting is like.

3. Notice the pressure of the writing strokes. Some folks press hard as they write so that if you were blind, you could probably read it all by just feeling it. Others write lightly. You can tell because the marks on the paper will be a lot lighter, and you might not even feel anything on the other side. According to graphologists, the "hard pressers" are the ones who have high energy, emotionally. It could mean they are sensual, intense, or vigorous. The "average pressers" are supposedly calm and grounded. They have great memory skills and great perception. The "light pressers" are supposedly introverts or those who vibe with low energy.

4. Notice the slant of the writing strokes. When it comes to cursive most folks will write with a slant to one side or the other. You can focus on the letters that have hoops on top, like, h, b, and d to figure out which sort of "slanter" you're dealing with. The "right slanters" are those who are happy to write, and they write fast and with energy. According to graphologists, this means they are confident and assertive. The "left slanter" is not willing to write or is hiding their emotions. According to graphologists, these writers don't cooperate as well as those who slant right. A "no slant" writer apparently has their emotions in control. However, these points may not necessarily apply to people who are left-handed.

5. Check out the baseline of the handwriting. Besides collecting several samples, you will need to go a step further by making sure they're not written on lined sheets. Often, folks won't write in a straight line if there are no lines on the paper. Using a ruler-straight

across your collection of handwriting samples, you can compare the angle of each written sentence. According to graphologists, writing upward shows a happy, upbeat, optimistic mood. Writing downward could mean fatigue or plain discouragement. If the writing is wavy, meaning up and down, it could mean the writer is uncertain, unstable, or unskilled.

6. Notice the letter sizes. When the writer uses small letters, it might mean they are introverted, reclusive, or thrifty. Large letters imply an outgoing, friendly, and extroverted nature.

7. Look at the space between words and letters. If the handwriting makes use of all the space it can, keeping things close together, then graphologists say the writer could be introverted or conscious about themselves. If they drag out the letters, it means they're independent and generous. As for the gaps between words, the closer they are, the more the writer likes crowds. Larger gaps apparently mean they have organized and clear thoughts.

8. Pay attention to the way the letters connect. Graphologists are of the opinion there is a wealth of information to be gleaned from the way a writer connects their letters. The trouble is, there are so many ways people write cursive, so it's hard to conclude on that. However, here are things which graphologists say: Writers who use garlands (curves shaped like cups, open on the top) are warm and strong; writers who use downward curves or arcades are more likely creative since these curves are dignified and slower to write; and writers who use threads, where the pen stroke gets increasingly lighter toward the word's end, or where there are trailing dots, are supposedly rushed and sloppy.

Another Way to Analyze Handwriting

Graphology isn't the only way to study handwriting. You can also make use of forensic document analysis, which is often mistaken for graphology. With this method, you can sometimes get hints about the person's sex, age, and other things like that, but it's not about figuring out their personality. What it's used for is to figure out forgery cases and compare handwriting with things like ransom notes or other evidence.

You must get all the samples you need voluntarily, with the same ink and the same paper. When you're practicing your analysis, you'll need your friends to write out the same, long text. Let them write it at least two times on two pieces of paper. When you're done collecting them, shuffle them together, and then you can go ahead with the methods that follow to match each pair accurately.

Forensic Document Analysis in Practice

1. Criminal investigators will use no less than three samples when dealing with a full letter, or they will use over 20 samples if they're working with a signature. Do the same.

2. Begin by looking for the differences among the letters. It's often a rookie mistake to start off looking for similarities, and then assume that it's the same writer without carrying out any further investigation. So, your first task is to look for all how the letters are different before you move on to looking for similarities.

3. Check out the baseline alignment by using the paper's line or a ruler under the writing when working with unlined paper. Some writers write below the line, while others write above. Some keep it level throughout, while others are up and down.

4. Track the space between each letter. This is the most objective way to make your comparisons. You'll need a ruler with a millimeter measure so that you can measure how much space is between words and letters. If there's a lot of difference in the spacing, then it could mean different writers. This is more than likely the case if there's one writing sample where the words are connected with strokes of the pen, and another sample has gaps.

5. Notice the relationship in height between the letters. Does the writer have a habit of writing their cursive Ks or Ls above the other

letters, or are they the same height? Often, this is a gauge much better than the loop width and letter slant.

6. Now, it's time to compare the shapes of the letter. There are lots of connectors, loops, curves, and letter endings that allow you to tell writers apart. The long and short of it is, you must check out a long piece of writing, and then compare that with a sample by someone else. First, look for the various versions of a letter in a single sample, so you can see what differences you can't rely on. No one writes the same way in the same document throughout. This way, you can rule out what you can't use. Next, look for a letter pretty much the same each time it shows up. People who write in cursive script will often either use the cursive version of the letter, a single, vertical stroke, or they will use that stroke but add in crossbars at the bottom and the top.

7. If you're feeling like Sherlock, you could deliberately seek signs of forgery by getting your friends to sign someone else's signature, and then put them all in a pile along with the original. Here are things to know with forgeries: Because the forger has to write slowly to copy the signature properly, there might be tremors and inconsistency in the thickness of the lines. Real signatures will have a change in line thickness as you speed up and slow down when you sign stuff. Also, look out for pen lifts (little gaps that appear in the signature) and inkblots, which naturally happen because the forger pauses or hesitates. You can find them at the beginning and end of the forged signature, or even between the letters. Also, attempt to sign your own signature no less than five times. You'll notice that it varies each time. If you notice there are two signatures too similar, matching every line and curve, then chances are one of them is the forgery.

Fun Graphology Facts

1. How high you put the bar in the letter "t" tells a lot about you. When the bar on the letter "t" is above the letters that precede and

follow it, it shows that you're optimistic. This is especially the case when the bar also has an upward slant to it. It means you're the person who reaches for your goal, no matter what. A low T-bar is not a good thing, especially if it is lower than the preceding and following letters. It means you underestimate your abilities, and you have no belief in yourself. You have low self-esteem, according to graphologists. If you have a downward slant to the T-bar, then that's even worse because it means you're depressed, according to Mike Mandel, graphologist, and hypnotist.

2. Lower zones are very telling. These are where the loops in a word go down and below the letters. Think of the small letter g, or y, for instance. According to Mike Mandel, the bigger the loop is, the more friends you need. The smaller the loop, the less you need friends in your life. The person who writes a g without a loop is really not even interested in close friends. They might have one, or none, and that's about it for them. They're okay with going it all alone when they need to. The bigger loop writer will need more people, or they cannot cope.

3. The size of your loop can reveal your sexual appetite. Again, those with large loops have a strong and healthy sexual appetite. They have a desire for stuff, money, food, and good things in life. Some don't have a loop when they write, but instead will draw the line straight down to a defined point, and then a curved hook back to the left. According to Mike Mandel, this is called the felon's claw. This appears in the handwriting of no less than 80 percent of felons in the American penitentiary system. Mandel says the felon's claw is a sure sign of manipulation and is a dangerous sign.

4. Graphologists do not judge people based on single letters or a pen slip. That's not enough to label them sane or psychotic. You also cannot judge them by stuff they've written on a board with chalk or a marker. They study people based on their usual handwriting, preferably written while they're sitting down, comfortable, writing on an unlined sheet of paper, and their preferred pencil or pen. The

goal is to get them to write so it mirrors, as close as possible, their usual method of writing.

5. "Weird handwriting equals weird people; weird lower zones, really weird person," says Mike Mandel. You have the felon's claw, but when the lower zone is something particularly weird, maybe with several weird loops, then you're dealing with someone with weird sex drives and sexual deviation to the most extreme degrees.

6. The signature you have is the personality you give the world, not your actual personality. It's not you. So, when you're going into a business or personal relationship with somebody, you want to know that their handwriting and their signature look similar. If they seem the same, that means this person is a straight shooter, and what you see is what you get when you deal with them. If the handwriting is legible, but the signature is just odd, and all over the place, they're holding something back about themselves and are not honest about who they are. It could be out of self-defense.

7. Signatures can let you know if a marriage is on the rocks. When a woman marries a man and takes on his last name, the space she puts between her first name and his last name shows how close or far apart they are in her mind.

8. A signature can also let you know if there's a problem between the writer and their family. If they sign with their first and last name, and they cross out their last name, they might justify it as a style or say that's how they've always crossed written it. However, on an unconscious level, they've crossed it out because they have no connection with their family or wish to distance themselves from their father or mother or some other relatives. Basically, they don't connect with their loved ones, according to Mike Mandel.

With proper training in graphology, you can learn the fascinating things about people based on their handwriting alone, and it could almost make you seem like you're psychic. But! There's no woo-woo going on here. It's all down to pure science and research.

Why Reading Handwriting is a Useful Skill

It would save us all so much trouble if we could figure out who people were based on thought bubbles that appeared on top of their heads. Imagine you knew everything someone was about, right from the get-go. You'd know whether you want to date them, so you'd never have to deal with needless heartbreak. You would know whether to trust a teenager to babysit your child or if you'd be better off taking them with you to work and risk annoying your boss and coworkers.

If you knew right from the start who you were dealing with, then you would know whether to lend them that money, or whether you want to enter into a business relationship with them. Sadly, there's no way to peer into the essence of someone (other than the eyes, perhaps). Therefore, you need to rely on *not just what they say*, but nonverbal cues and other things like handwriting.

When you have the professional knowledge that expert graphologists do, it can become a lot easier for you to figure out who you're dealing with. Again, I'm not suggesting you cancel someone based on the information you get from this book. I am saying, however, that you would be more cautious of who you're dealing with, and you probably would save yourself lost dollars and lost time.

Handwriting analysis can be useful when trying to figure out who to hire for a certain job, so you know you're going with the person who is likely to be more productive and less of a headache. It can be useful in understanding the people you're dealing with, and whether it's worth it to get into arguments with them or try to explain things to them. You may know a few people always looking for a fight, no matter what. There's just no reasoning with them. If you had the opportunity to assess their handwriting before engaging with them, and you knew of the science of graphology, you probably have saved yourself a headache or two. That's why handwriting analysis matters. It can help you understand people and make life a lot easier.

Chapter Seven: Mind-Reading with Neuro-Linguistic Programming

If you want to do a stellar job of reading other people's minds, then you should look to neuro-linguistic programming. To understand Neuro-linguistic programming (NLP), let's look at the three basic parts to the term. Neuro is short for neurology and is basically the physical, emotional, and mental aspects of brain function. Linguistic refers to the language you use, and how you engage in communication with others, and even more important, the way you communicate with you. Programming is the way your past thoughts, emotions, and experiences affect every aspect of your life. So, to summarize, NLP is the language of your mind.

NLP in Action

There are three key elements in NLP:
- Modeling
- Action
- Effective communication

If someone can figure out how someone else finishes their tasks, then they can copy that process, and they can also let others know how to finish those tasks.

Everyone has a view of reality that is personal. NLP practitioners will critically analyze their perspectives, and others' perspectives so that they can have a holistic view of an event or situation. Once you can grasp the variations in perspectives, you gain valuable information. There is no better way to learn this information than by taking advantage of your mind and body, immersing yourself in these experiences.

NLP Mind Reading

The process of NLP's mind-reading involves assuming that you're well aware of what someone else feels or thinks in any particular situation. The truth is no one could ever know the entirety of your thoughts and emotions. They may have a close match, but not the full picture. So, if you have ever felt certain you know how someone feels or what they're thinking, then you're mind-reading –a tricky thing that can get you into trouble.

In reading minds, you must account for the parts of the other person's experience which you can actually verify with your own senses. Once you assume you know every little thought in their head, then you forget that thought you know it all is actually your thought, and not necessarily a reflection of objective reality.

How to Mind Read

Sometimes, we believe we know what other people's intentions are based on the way they act or don't act. We could assume that someone is really into us, or that they're not, or that they're out to get us. Reading minds with NLP reveals that "the map is not the territory," as one NLP presupposition says. We've all made mistakes when it comes to jumping to conclusions about the way others feel or about why they chose to do certain things. With ourselves, we judge based on intention. With others, we judge based on actions.

We also forget that no one is a mind reader in the *actual sense of the term.* We somehow expect our significant other to know without using our words that we're mad because they forgot to take the trash out again, or that we appreciate the amazing dinner they put together. This can cause a lot of trouble, because if both parties expect the other to somehow always know what's on their mind without checking in, then there's a lot of room for misunderstanding.

How CAN You Read People's Minds?

We need to discuss accessing cues. When people are thinking about something, they often will show some subtle action that lets them activate the right representation of what they're thinking. They might move their eyes, change their position, breathe differently, make certain gestures, change their intonation, and so on.

These behaviors are useful cues you can keep track of, so you know how they might be about to respond to an event or to you. These cues won't tell you the meat of what they're thinking, but it will let you know *how* they think.

For instance, if you've ever seen someone who's making faces, scratching an itch, out of breath, using onomatopoeic sounds, or making familiar hand gestures, you may not ascribe any meaning to these actions all on their own. However, you can tell what actual process is going on with their mind when they do these things.

As you practice NLP, you will decipher these behaviors easily, and this will put you in a position to affect the way others think. Here are patterns which you should know:

1. Auditory mode accessing cues: Here, the eyes and head lean sideways, all gestures happen at ear level, and the breathing is diaphragmatic. The speed of their speech will switch between fast and slow, and their intonation will go up and down.

2. Kinesthetic mode accessing cues: Here, the eyes and head are down. All gestures are directed to the body, and the breathing is down in the belly. Their speech gets slower, and their intonation goes deeper.

3. Visual mode accessing cues: Here, the eyes and head are up. All gestures will be made upward, or above the shoulders. They breathe in the upper part of the respiratory system (the lungs), and their eyes are halfway closed. Also, the voice goes higher in pitch and speed.

Practice Accessing Cues

You're going to need a friend for this one! When you're done, have them let you know what you did after each step. You want them to pay attention to what happened with your facial expression, posture, gestures, breathing, and tone of voice.

1. Recall something fun you did or were a part of.

2. Pay attention to the physical sensations you had from that experience.

3. Now, let the feelings go.

4. Next, think about the pictures tied to your experience.

5. Now, let the pictures go.

6. Next, pay attention to the sounds tied to your experience.

7. Now, let the sounds go.

Now, time to switch places.

Who Uses NLP?

NLP is used in self-help and therapy circles, and in complicated ways such as AI banking technology to discover whether people who have never taken a loan or even owned a bank account are likely to make good on their debts. It's that amazing.

In NLP, the map is not the territory because it often will show you the stark differences between reality and belief. Each person will act based on their perspective of things, not pure objectivity.

There are as many maps as there are people. So, it's the NLP therapists' job to figure out what your map is like, and the way this map may affect your thoughts and actions.

The therapist uses NLP to help people figure out their behavioral and thinking patterns, aspirations, and emotional state. Armed with this information, they can help their patients to do better at the skills that benefit them and develop ways of dropping the habits that are unproductive.

Hypnotic Mind Reading Techniques

1. The Delayed Echo: Most people enjoy talking about themselves, and as they do, you invariably learn something about them. You learn things like the name of their cousin's cat, what they did in Cape Town during the summer, and all sorts of other info. Often, they mention them in passing, so they eventually forget they did mention it. Here's where you get to "read minds" by paying close attention. What must you do? Remember every fact. Do your best not to draw their attention to the information they shared. Right away, talk about anything else besides that bit of info. Give it about five minutes, when they must have forgotten what they told you. Finally, mention the cat or holiday experiences, but use different phrases and words from the ones they used to share that info with you. This way, you're literally their delayed echo. As you use different language, you seem like you somehow picked up on their experiences, like you had a crystal ball or something.

2. Flattery: People find it flattering when you can see them for who they are on the inside. As you describe them, your description might not be accurate, but often those traits you're talking about will be relatable and easy to identify with. Am I advocating you lie to someone about them? No. It matters that your flattery is strictly founded upon truth. This is not only honest, but the listener is also likely to believe you because of it. I will give a few examples here, but please remember that they work particularly with Western

166

culture. When dealing with people from other cultures, they might not work - or be acceptable. General traits you can assume of someone include friendliness, hard-working, smart, positive, reliable, resourceful, loyal, and honest. Traits you can assume are true of females are helpful, perceptive, underappreciated, intuitive, sensitive. As for males, you can assume their traits include, rational, independent, confident, excellent problem-solving skills, practical.

3. **Covering All Possibilities (CAP):** This "mind-reading technique" is like the previous one, except you pick two opposing traits. You want to make sure you choose general traits, not facts that can be quantified and thus disproven. For instance, you could say, "You love to hear people out, but sometimes you can get a bit impatient." This general statement could apply to anyone. They will be accepting of it because you've first highlighted the positive side to them, which takes the sting out of your negative observation. Therefore, a lot of horoscope readings seem to be oh so accurate. In making these statements, you might want to add humor to make it even easier for the listener to accept.

4. **The Barnum Effect:** This is named after the famous circus leader, PT Barnum. Here, you make a very specific statement, yet, it's one that could apply to almost anyone. You begin by making a general statement, and then you observe their reaction. Based on this reaction, you can move on to more specific statements. Here's how that would work: "You're a kind person — [wait for reaction] — no matter how bad things turn out; you always look for the best in the experience. You tend to find opportunities where others don't and make the best of what you've got." Now, let's try this again, but with the presumption that the reaction is negative: "You're not afraid to dream — [wait for reaction] — but you're also very practical. You don't let your dreams remain dreams. You love to root everything you do firmly in reality, and that's why you'll go places." If you're very astute, you'll notice those examples used both the flattery method and the CAP method. Now, you want to make sure you also use negative personality traits when describing them, so you

don't appear to be pandering or making absurd leaps. You could start off saying, "You tend to be hard on yourself," or "You're quite talented at keeping grudges indefinitely," or "There are things you've done in the past that you regret deeply."

5. The Seven Ages of Man: This is also called "universal experiences." With this technique, you're leaning heavily on the things we've all gone through at various points in our lives. Basically, you seek what people may be going through at the moment based on their age. Remember that the examples to follow are based on Western culture. Sometimes, certain examples are considered out of style, so you want to remember that. Here are the seven ages of man:

> 18 to 22: At this time, you leave home, and you explore many lifestyles. You want to prove that you can make it in the world of adults.

> 22 to 30: You're either off seeking an adventure or building a nest. You're either avoiding commitment or actively seeking it out. Also, career matters a lot .

> 30 to 35: You're re-evaluating everything you've done with life. If you were all about adventure, you think of settling down. If you were all about building a nest, you wonder what your commitments may be keeping you from.

> 33 to 45: The infamous midlife crises. You either finally break away from your commitments to seek new adventures, or you finally settle down to have the family you've been running away from. You feel, erroneously, that you're running out of time and that life is passing you by, so you want to make the most of it.

> 45 to 55: Your career is wrapping up. It all comes down to how well you handle your midlife crises. If you did well, then that means you'll have experienced a wonderful rebirth. If not, you'll feel like there's no hope, and you'd be disappointed in yourself.

55 to 75: You're done with work. Now you have more time, resources, and freedom to travel, explore, and have fun. You have fewer responsibilities. However, health might become an issue. Your friends pass on, and you start feeling lonely.

Armed with these facts, you can get backdoor access to someone's thoughts. You may not totally know their age, but you can make a rough estimate and read them based on that.

Chapter Eight: Dark Psychology — Recognizing the Dark Triad

"Some men just want to watch the world burn." Remember that quote by Alfred Pennyworth? Well, it's spot on. There are those who are downright difficult to live with, no matter what you do. They might be arrogant, with a penchant for being mercurial and domineering, but you can work with them to help them improve focusing on their strengths and neutralizing the less-than-desirable traits they have.

However, there's this other class of people who live only for the view of a world set on fire. They have toxic, damaging behaviors, poisoning and destroying those around them, in every way possible. These people's three traits are the sole components of the "Dark Triad," a term coined by psychologists. Here are the traits:

- Narcissism
- Machiavellianism
- Psychopathy

Now let's describe each one as best we can.

Narcissism: The word "narcissism" is from Greek mythology. There was a hunter named Narcissus, who had fallen deeply in love with his reflection, which he'd spotted by chance in a pool of water.

He fell so deeply in love he fell into the water and drowned. Narcissists are selfish, lacking in empathy, arrogant, boastful, and overly sensitive to criticism.

Machiavellianism: This world exists thanks to Niccolo Machiavelli, an Italian politician and diplomat from the 16th century. He wrote a book called "The Prince" in 1513, and it was basically awash with praise for deceit and cunning in diplomatic matters. Machiavellian traits include manipulation, duplicity, self-interest, and a lack of morality and emotion.

Psychopathy: The traits of psychopathy include antisocial behavior, lack of remorse and empathy, and being volatile and manipulative. Remember that there's a difference between being an actual psychopath and simply having psychopathic traits. Often, psychopaths engage in criminal violence.

All these personalities are incredibly difficult to read. The narcissist, for instance, has mastered the art of seeming sincere and true when needed. They're a master at reflecting whatever you want to see. So how do you spot these people?

How to Spot Your Neighborhood Narcissist

The narcissist oozes charm like no one else. A study showed that you could only see through their smoke and mirrors by the seventh time you meet them. Falling in love with them can ruin you. Literally, they will take a greatly confident person with high self-esteem and turn them into unrecognizable versions of themselves. Here are the hallmarks of Narcissistic Personality Disorder:

1. A grand sense of self-importance, where they overhype their talents, skills, and achievements. The narcissist wants you to know how awesome they are. If they haven't actually achieved anything yet, they will brag to you about how they're going to. They need to be constantly appreciated, recognized, and validated.

2. Dreams and aspirations of unlimited success, power, beauty, brilliance, or "ideal" love.

3. A need for constant, excess admiration. As for the narcissist, their job is to talk about themselves, and your job is to listen. They won't ask about you. When you do chip in something about your own life, they're quick to turn the spotlight back on themselves. This can quickly get annoying and boring. On the flip side, narcissists are masters of charm. They're successful, beautiful, or talented, and these are things that keep us all enamored with them. However, those narcissists are great at the art of seduction and can make you feel greatly loved and admired. Until they're bored.

4. A belief they are unique and special and can only be understood by those who are unique or special; in other words, people they perceive to be of high status. They also believe they should only ever associate with these "special" people (or organizations.) This is why they'll name-drop, only patronize the best restaurants, and have the most expensive toys. It's all just to hide how empty they are inside.

5. A lack of empathy for other people's emotions and needs. There are people who lack empathy but aren't narcissists. However, this trait is essential when identifying the narcissist in your midst. Pay attention to their face and body language when you recount a sad story. They can be rude, refuse to listen to you, decide for you without seeking your input, and so on. These are only little things but put all these actions together, and you'll notice you might be dealing with a narc.

6. A sense of entitlement to special treatment and constant compliance with their every wish. As far as they're concerned, the world revolves around them. If it doesn't, then someone had better fix it. They don't think the rules apply to them. Nothing is ever their fault.

7. A tendency to take advantage of people and exploit them to get their own personal gains. They take and take, but they don't give. When they do, there's a motive.

8. A belief that others envy them, and never-ending of clothes they perceive, is doing better than they are.

9. An air of arrogance.

How to Spot Your Master Machiavellian

To summarize the personality of the Machiavellian, you only need to look at two quotes from the book, The Prince. "A wise ruler ought never to keep faith when, by doing so, it would be against his interests." How about this other lovely little gem: "A prince never lacks good reasons to break his promise."? Machiavellian believes that honesty is not needed if it would make more sense to use force, deceit, and treachery instead.

The Machiavellian is a master manipulator. They are duplicitous, constantly deceiving people to get what they want. They have no sense of morals and consider other people nothing more than steppingstones to get where they need to. The Machiavellian believes that anyone who allows themselves to be used most likely deserved it.

Sure, we can all be dishonest every now and then, but for the Machiavellian, this is just another Tuesday. The "High Mach" sincerely believes in this quote by Groucho Marx, "Sincerity is everything. If you can fake that, you've got it made." It was only a joke, but don't tell the High Mach that. Here are five traits you can spot them by:

1. The High Mach does best in social situations and careers where the rules are not set in stone, allowing them to get creative with boundaries.

2. For the High Mach, holding a cynical outlook on life and being emotionally detached helps them to keep their impulses in check, and teaches them to be patient in their opportunism.

3. The High Mach believes in using such tactics as guilt, charm, self-disclosure, friendliness, and, when needed, pressure. Anything to get their way.

4. The High Mach would much rather be subtle about their tactics. They masquerade as being friendly, they pour on the charm,

make you feel guilty, and share stuff with you about themselves when they must, to give you a false sense of solidarity. This way, they can conceal their actual intentions and give themselves room for plausible deniability if you catch them at their game. They're not above pressure and threats when needed.

5. Most people would rather have the High Mach on their side with negotiations, debates, and other competitive situations. However, no one wants to have them as colleagues, friends, or spouses.

How to Spot Your Sadistic Psychopath

This is the psychopath, summed up in a Ted Bundy quote: "I don't feel guilty for anything. I feel sorry for people who feel guilt." Fortunately, for most of us, we need not deal with psychopaths in our everyday lives. However, if you have to, it helps to know the person you're dealing with. Here are various traits noticeable in this personality:

1. Manipulation is considered "high art" to them. Perhaps the psychopath is the grandmaster of manipulation. They know how to suck you into their lies, make you see what they want you to see, and nothing more. Even when you know the truth, and it niggles at you in the back of your mind, they know how to make you desperate to believe their version of events.

2. They are experts at reading people. The psychopath has an uncanny ability to size you up in just an instant at your first meeting. They hardly ever get it wrong. Best believe they will explore every weakness about you they can. Somehow, they can home in on your soft spot and take advantage of it. Whether you've got a big heart, or you are all about a big score, a quick and easy win, or you're just gullible, they'll know, and they'll use it. When you're in a personal relationship with a psychopath, they will learn everything about you they can, and then they will turn that knowledge into an arsenal of deadly weapons they expertly wield against you, cutting you down

bit by bloody bit, until there's nothing left of you. Sounds dramatic, but that's the psychopath.

3. They are charming. Not that you should be wary of charming people; this just means the psychopath can instantly disarm you with charm. That's their thing. They don't even have to try.

4. They will blindside you with pain. They have all this information on you, but they won't use it right away. They're happy to wait and use it against you in the future when they feel it will deal you the most damage. People are often shocked when the psychopath finally strikes, and the mask comes off.

5. They will say whatever you want to hear. If you've been in a relationship with them for a while, it can be shocking when you learn they've only been using you, telling you what you want to hear. Often family and friends of psychopathic murderers are shocked because they never gave even a hint of evil.

6. They do not have a conscience. They have no moral compass. They're ready to act in whatever ways they please to get what they want, or just to add more fire to the flames. It's not just that they do heinous things. They relish being terrible. There's no rhyme or reason for the joy that they feel in destroying everything around them.

7. They cannot relate to fear. They're incapable of it. They might feel it, but they don't know how to automatically detect it, let alone respond to it.

8. Their work history is inconsistent. You'd be hard-pressed to find them working a job for too long. They might get bored and move on, or they might fire themselves. Whichever the case, they're exceptionally good at explaining away their inconsistency with work that it's easy to believe their stories without further questioning.

9. They have dead, lifeless eyes. A quick Google search for famous psychopaths will show you that. It's almost as if there is no soul behind those eyes. Even when they're upbeat, charming, and seemingly happy, those eyes stay flat.

10. They talk in a monotone voice; you can hardly get them to speak louder. Also, since the psychopath has no actual emotions, their speech doesn't have that natural rise and fall that others have.

11. They have no empathy. They cannot relate to someone else's pain, and they couldn't be bothered to do so. The only emotions they will respond to are extreme displays of fear and anger, and that's only because they want to exploit these emotions, just for kicks.

12. The psychopath is arrogant and entitled. Keep in mind that regardless of their upbringing, whether they grew up privileged or disadvantaged, they all have that sense of entitlement, and everything they do or say comes from that place.

13. The psychopath doesn't care for rules and doesn't play by them. They will blatantly flaunt them, just for the fun of getting away with it to show how they are above it all.

14. When they do get caught, they don't care about the consequences of their actions. They literally treat getting caught as just the cost of doing business. It doesn't stop them from doing more awful things to others.

15. They will lie to your face without pause. They'll weave fantastic tales to draw you in. And you'll let them. You'll buy into it. Not because you're stupid, but because they're skilled liars.

16. As kids, they are usually violent toward their siblings or pets. They kill animals, just for fun. Where the sociopath learns to become that way, the psychopath is born, not made.

17. Finally, the psychopath is all about the fun of controlling others. They love to dominate and have everyone under their thumb. That's all they live for.

The dark triad of narcissism, Machiavellianism, and psychopathy is something we could all do without. You'll find that there is some overlap in traits with these personalities. They can be damaging and toxic with personal relationships, where you're more than likely to let down your guard and let them in.

I read a story about a woman dealing with identity fraud. She's had her bank accounts and credit cards compromised. The one person who supported her through this was her fiancé, who had moved in with her. She was in touch with the FBI in hopes of solving the case. She had to deal with stress and anxiety, and this got no better as the authorities were having trouble tracking down the culprit.

Her fiancé was a stalwart and staunch support for her in these times. He comforted her. He bought her gifts. He paid the monthly rent for her - from money she'd given him. After months, her landlord came to confront her for not paying her rent for several months in a row. She then realized that her fiancé had been stashing her rent money for himself, using it only to buy her gifts. It was difficult to come to terms with her being in love with a manipulative, gaslighting narcissist.

There are tales even worse than this one. A quick google search will show you countless experiences and encounters people have had with them of the dark triad. This is why it is more important than ever to learn how to spot these people. You cannot read them the way you'd read regular folk, but certain traits will show up often, letting you know to put a lot of distance between you and them.

These people are callous, and you need to protect yourself. Do not reason with them, do not attempt to get them to change, and do not try to win them over. It may seem like you're making progress, but I promise you they're only playing a game with you; you will lose – and lose hard. If you suspect you might be dealing with someone with a dark triad personality, then the first thing to do is seek the help of a professional psychotherapist. Please do not walk up to them to confront them. That would do nothing except put you on their radar or encourage them to move up the timeline of whatever evil they have planned for you.

Please be willing to share your experience with others. It does no good trying to cover it up. That's just one way to deny the validity of your experience, and it does no one any good. You can educate yourself more on these dark triad personalities so that if you meet them, you're well equipped to handle them if you are where you can't avoid them.

Chapter Nine: Signs of Lies and Deception

Everyone can lie. A lot of us do – there's no use denying that. It's been studied, and scientists have found that you're likely to tell a couple of lies a day. If everyone lies, and lies that often, then it becomes important to tell when they do so.

How to go about reading people to see if they're deceitful is to see what they're usually like when they're honest. For instance, if you asked them, "What's your name?" you could use that to observe where they look, how their voice sounds, and how they breathe. You could follow up with similar questions that there's no use lying about, such as where they're from (assuming they have no reason to deny where they're from.)

Once you've got their baseline, you have only to look for changes in facial expressions, bodily movements, the content of speech, and tone of voice. It's not that simple, though. For instance, they may be fidgety, but only because they're nervous, not lying. Their voice may crack, but only out of anxiety, not because they're fibbing. There are lots of reasons they could seem uneasy when they're answering your questions.

Lying Hands

When you're talking to a liar, they will often make hand gestures after they've spoken, instead of before or during their speech. The reason for this is that the mind is working hard to piece together a story, see if the story is being bought, and what they can do to beef it up if it isn't. So, instead of the usual gesture made before or during a statement, you get one that comes after they've spoken.

There was a study carried out by the University of Michigan in 2015, where the researchers considered 120 video clips of high-profile court cases. They wanted to decipher how people act when they're honest, versus when they're lying. They found that the liars would often use both hands to gesture, more often than those being honest. It's worth mentioning that 40 percent of the clips with liars showed them using both hands to gesture, compared to 25 percent of the honest people.

Another remarkable thing about hands and liars is that when they're dishonest, the liars will unconsciously have their palms facing away This signifies that they're not telling you the full story, they're hiding how they feel, or they're flat-out lying. They might put their hands underneath the table and keep them there. They might simply keep them in their pockets.

Itchy and Fidgety

When someone cocks their head to the side, moves their body in rocking back and forth motion, or shuffles their feet, they might be deceiving you about something. As the liar lies, there are fluctuations in their body's autonomic nervous system. The ANS deals with bodily functions and can play a part in giving away the liar. When you're nervous, you will feel fluctuations in your nervous system, interpreting them as tingle or itches, causing you to fidget. There's also research spearheaded by R. Edward Geiselman, a psychology professor at UCLA, which shows that when people are dishonest, they engage in "grooming behaviors." They play with their hair, check underneath their nails for dirt, and things like that.

Giving Face

When someone's lying to you, they might either look away or stare at a critical moment. They move their eyes about because they're trying to come up with something to say. Geiselman's research also found that people tend to look away for a bit when they lie. The 2015 University of Michigan study also found that liars stare a lot more than those who are truthful. Interestingly, 70 percent of the clips they viewed showed the liars staring directly at the people they lied to.

Even with all these studies, there is still room for debate about eye contact and lying. Plos One published a study in 2012 that discredited the idea that people look in a certain direction as they lie. Sure, maybe you might read too much of nothing into someone else's behavior, but you cannot discount the eyes, as they often hold the truth.

When someone is holding back information from you, then they might roll their lips back, so they almost aren't visible. It's often because they're holding back facts or trying to keep their emotions in check.

The UCLA study showed that someone lying to you would often purse their lips when you ask them questions that they find sensitive. The pursed lips say they don't want to talk about the subject at the moment.

Skin complexion also gives liars away. When someone is talking, and they go white or pale, it could mean that they're not truthful, as blood rushes out of their face.

Are they dry or sweaty? The autonomic nervous system will often cause a liar to sweat in their T-area (the forehead, upper lip, chin, and areas around the mouth.) They might also have to contend with dry eyes and a dry mouth. You can tell by observing how often they squint or blink, and whether they swallow hard, or bite or lick their lips.

The Voice Behind the Words

When you're dealing with a nervous person, it's not unusual for the vocal cords to tighten up. This is a natural response to being in a stressful situation, and it causes the voice to become high-pitched. There might also be a creak in their voice. When someone clears their throat in these situations, it could be because they're trying to deal with the uncomfortably tight muscles, and that could also be a sign that they're lying.

If you notice that they've suddenly turned up the volume, maybe they're getting defensive about something. Whether or not this means they're lying depends on the context.

The Words

When someone has to say stuff like, "Let me be honest," "Trust me," "I want to be truthful to you," then they might be working a little too hard to make you think they're honest. Be mindful of judging them based on these phrases, though, as this isn't a hard-and-fast rule.

There's a little something known as "vocal fill" - filler words like "like," "ah," "uh," and "um," among others. It's often a sign of deception. When people talk like this, they might be trying to give themselves more time to come up with a good lie.

Unless you're part of the dark triad of personalities, we're all, mostly, not natural liars. Because of this, we sometimes spill the tea without meaning to. Sometimes, a person might slip up by saying, "I kissed her — no, wait, I mean she kissed me," or "I was on the I-95 as at then — wait, no, I was actually grabbing a bite to eat." You're dealing with someone who doesn't have the best memory - or, you're dealing with a liar.

Do they speak in sentence fragments? If they're not completing their sentences, then they might be spinning a story on the spot.

Tips for Spotting Liars

Notice when they do not refer to themselves in the story. When people are honest, they will often use the pronoun "I" to let you know what they did. "I kicked off my shoes before I unlocked the door and stepped into his house. As I walked in, I noticed a strange-looking man with a greenish pallor seated on the rocking chair to my right. Since it was a bit dark, I didn't notice the weapon in his hand sooner. I felt nothing for a few seconds, and then the pain overwhelmed me. But I was able to fire off a couple of shots at him before I went down." Notice the use of the many pronouns, "I," here.

When people are untruthful, they will often speak in a way that reduces attention to themselves. They speak with the passive voice as they describe what happened. They'll say, "The door was unlocked," rather than "I unlocked the door." They'll say, "the man was shot," rather than "I fired off a couple of shots."

Another way they try to take the attention off themselves is by using the word "you" instead of "I". For instance, if asked, "Can you tell me why you shot him?" they might reply, "You know, you can't really be too careful. You do your best to make sure that no one gets hurt, and sometimes when things are really dangerous, that means you have to take the most extreme course of action."

Sometimes, whether they're recounting the experience in oral or written form, they will omit pronouns. "Took off shoes. The door unlocked, so, walked into the house. Man with green skin and gun sitting on the rocking chair. Boom! Gun goes off."

Notice the verb tense they use. If they're honest, they will use the past tense to describe events. When someone is lying, they often talk about the events like they're happening in the present – a surefire sign that they're rehearsing their lies. As you listen, notice the precise points at which they switch from past tense to present tense.

If they answer your questions with questions, something's up. As I mentioned before, we're not born liars. A liar doesn't want to lie; there's a chance they'll get caught. They might answer your question with a question so they need not provide an answer. If you asked, "Why did you shoot him?" they might ask, "Why would I shoot someone if they weren't a threat?" or, "Do I look like I just go in guns blazing to you?"

Beware of equivocation. If they avoid answering your questions by using vague and uncertain expressions, and weak modifiers, then you want to be on high alert. I'm talking about words like "maybe," "sort of," "think," "perhaps," "guess," "about," "approximately," "could," "might," and so on. These expressions give them some wiggle room to back out of statements they make when confronted in the future.

Also, watch out for noncommittal verbs like "assume," "figure," "believe," "guess," and so on, and vague qualifiers like "more or less," or "you might say."

Oaths are a red flag. The liar will do their best to convince you that what they say is "God's honest truth." You must believe them, because "cross my heart" they'd never lie. You'll hear, "I swear." Sometimes that's not enough, so they'll say, "I swear on my honor," or "I swear on my mother's grave." Conversely, someone who is honest does not feel the need to convince you, since they are confident of what they're saying and certain that the facts will stand up for them.

Euphemisms are also red flags. Almost every language will give an alternate term for most actions and situations. Guilty liars will use vague or mild words, rather than synonyms explicit in nature. They do this to make you listen more favorably and downplay whatever they did. So if they say "missing" when they could have said "stolen," replace the word "took" with "borrowed," say "bumped" rather than "hit," or claim to have "warned" someone instead of saying "threatened," then you're likely dealing with a liar.

A liar will allude to actions. They'll never really say they did them. They'll say, "I try to make sure I water the lawn every day," rather than "I water the lawn every day." Or, "I decided that we were going to take a walk through the woods." Well, did they walk through the woods?" They might say, "I needed to go over the books with her." Did they? All these are allusions, and they're not saying definitively that they did –or did not – do these things.

Liars will give too little detail. They want to keep their statements short and sweet. Few liars have the imagination to create detailed stories of things that never happened. Besides, the fewer the details, the better for the liar, so they don't get caught when contradicting evidence pops up. Now, when telling the truth, details that seem inconsequential will pop up, because they're trying to pull from long term memory, which stores many things besides this main event. Some liars know this and will go the whole nine yards to craft a lot of detail in their story. Better ones will genuinely convince themselves of these details, accepting them as true, so you have no choice but to read them as honest. These are likely a part of the dark triad.

Pay attention to the narrative balance of their story. When narrating, you have the prologue, the main event, and the epilogue or aftermath. When someone is telling the truth, the prologue will be about ⅕ to ¼ part of the narrative, the main event will be ⅖ to ⅗ of the narrative, and the aftermath will be about ¼ of it all. If these parts feel longer than needed, they may be chock full of lies.

Notice how many words are in a sentence. This is known as the "mean length of utterance" or MLU, which is calculated by adding up the number of words in an entire statement, and then dividing the total by the number of sentences in the statement. Mostly, people speak in sentences of about 10 to 15 words each. When they're anxious, they will speak in sentences noticeably longer or shorter.

Remember: do not focus on body language only. True, there are certain body movements that would allude to the possibility that you're witnessing the birth of a fairy tale, but some of the classic lying cues given by the body aren't tied to lying alone. Sometimes, with the eyes, it's possible that they're only thinking of trying to get to their long-term memory when they look in a "lying direction." This is based on research by psychologist Howard Ehrlichman, who's been studying eye movement since the 1970s. Body language is useful for seeking out lies, but you can't depend on them alone.

Pay attention to the right signals. While there are valid cues for spotting lies, the trouble is these cures can be very weak ways to detect deception. The most accurate cues you should focus on are vagueness, where the speaker is not adding in significant details; vocal uncertainty, where they seem unsure of what they're saying; indifference, where they act bored, shrug, or have no facial expression, hiding the emotions they feel; and overthinking, where they seem like they're working on a difficult calculus equation in their heads, instead of telling a story that should be easy to recount *if it were true.*

Have them tell you their story in reverse. This is a more active and better way to uncover their lies. There is research that has shown when you ask people to walk you back through their story, instead of in chronological order, it's easier to tell when they're lying. This is because the brain now has double the work, and is so focused on getting it right that it can't be bothered with trying to cover up verbal and nonverbal cues that suggest deception. It's a lot more difficult to lie than it is to tell the truth, and making the brain work harder will make the behavioral cues for lying more obvious.

Liars have to spend a lot of mental energy formulating the lie, making it difficult to keep track their behavior AND the way you respond to them as they lie to you. This takes a lot out of them, and so when you add in something taxing to the mix, they will crack.

Trust your gut. Sometimes, your gut reaction is the best thing to go on. There was a study where 72 participants were shown clips of interviews with crime suspects, who were just actors. Some of the said suspects were guilty of stealing $100 from a bookshelf. Yet, every suspect was instructed to tell the interviewer they hadn't stolen the money. The participants only identified the liars 43 percent of the time, and the honest people 48 percent of the time.

The researchers assessed the unconscious and automatic responses to the suspect by making use of their inherent behavioral reaction time. They found that often, the participants would unconsciously connect the words "deceitful" and "dishonest" with suspects who were guilty, while associating the words "honest" and "valid" with the suspects who told the truth. This means we have an intuitive notion of whether we're being lied to.

The question then becomes, why aren't we good at knowing when someone feeds us lies? Our conscious responses mess with our instinctual associations. So, rather than depend on the gut, people would rather focus on the behaviors stereotypically and sometimes erroneously associated with lying.

No Universal Sign for Lies

To catch a liar, first understand that these behaviors researched are nothing more than cues that *might* mean deceit is in play. Rather than looking at the usual lying signs, notice the subtler behaviors that might indicate dishonesty. If you need to, you can make it even harder for them to lie by adding pressure, asking the speaker to tell you the story again, but backward. Above all, and this bears repeating, trust your gut. It will save you needless pain and trouble. Your gut will not and can never steer you wrong if you do not let your head get in the way.

Chapter Ten: Spotting Flirters and Seducers

Flirting is such an amazing thing, especially when you're the object of attention, and the other person is just as into you as you are into them. The trouble is figuring out if they're just nice, or if really something go on that you could both explore. Maybe you're the one person who can never tell when someone is hitting on them or flirting with them. Or, you might have a problem distinguishing when someone is nice from when they're flirty. Either way, it's okay. After this chapter, you'll never have to wonder again.

Let's Play "Spot the Flirt"

Sign #1: They're different around you. Some people are overt flirters. They're into you, and you'll know it — or at least, everyone else who isn't clueless will know. Other people simply change the way they act around you and hope you notice. Pay attention to whether they laugh louder, get the quiet, joke, and talk a lot more, or become a bumbling, nervous wreck.

Sign #2: They connect with your eyes and hold them. You can tell by looking at their eyes whether they're flirting with you. There are studies that show when someone holds your gaze for long periods, it either results in feelings of affection, or it means the affection is already there. If they're making eye contact with you, and they're not looking anywhere else, then it's likely that they think you're attractive.

Sign #3: They're constantly glancing at you. Some people don't hold eye contact. They glance at you. The difference between a regular glance and a flirty one is if they glance a lot and catch your eye often.

Sign #4: There's a smile that's for you alone – no one else. If someone is flirting with you, they'll look at you with different eyes than they do others. You'll find those twin pools glinting with a heartwarming softness. If they were smiling before you locked eyes, the smile grows in brightness or intensity.

Sign #5: They make a habit of teasing you. There's nothing straightforward about flirting like this, but it happens often. People who flirt this way are trying not to be too obvious about it. They will gently poke fun at you, and offer you compliments indirectly, hoping against hope you take the hint. This teasing differs from bullying or insulting, so if you feel like they're putting you down, or you're uncomfortable, then maybe it's time to walk away.

Sign #6: They fidget with their clothes. Sometimes, they might fiddle with their outfit or hair, jewelry, even hands. Whatever they can get within reach. It often means they're nervous because you, their crush, are with them. They can barely contain themselves around you.

Sign #7: They try to discover if you're single in the sneakiest way they can. You may have heard them say something like, "Wow, does your girlfriend have any idea how lucky she is?" Or they'll say, "How in the world are you still single?" They're trying to find out if they stand a chance with you, or you've already taken, but they don't want to be upfront about it.

Sign #8: They always try to get a laugh out of you. They want you to relax and be at ease with them, so they'll joke, do silly things, anything to get you giggling and wondering if a life with them one would be full of laughter.

Sign #9: They think you're hilarious in a good way. You'll find that they laugh at every joke you make even when it's not that great. They want you to know that they like you, and they appreciate you.

Sign #10: They maintain open body language with you. They'll want to be closer to you, and to facilitate that, they will keep their body language open to you. They want you to know, on an unconscious level, that they are at ease in your presence. If you notice they're facing you, leaning in, and their feet and knees are pointed right at you, then they're probably flirting.

Sign #11: They'll react first to your posts on social media. If they keep liking and commenting on your stuff, it could only mean they want to get your attention, especially when they like EVERYTHING.

Sign #12: You notice they check you out. You know you can scope someone out surreptitiously; if you catch them doing that to you, then it's pretty obvious that they're attracted to you and trying to flirt.

Sign #13: They touch you in subtle ways. Those accidental touches aren't so accidental. They might give you a quick pat on the shoulder, graze your arm, or attempt to brush your feet or hands if you're seated at the bar or at a table. These parts of the body are sensitive and will often cause you to instinctively consider whether you're attracted to them or not.

Sign #14: They do their best to get in your line of sight. When you're in the same space together, notice if they somehow always wind up in your line of sight, or if they somehow are always close to you, but not quite. They probably want to get to know you but aren't brave enough to start a conversation or want you to make the first move.

Sign #15: They fidget suggestively. Here, if they're playing with their wine glass, or its stem, or whatever, but moving their hands in almost hypnotic, deliberate strokes as they focus on you, chances are they're interested and trying to flirt with you.

Sign #16: They keep pointing out their flaws; an odd way to flirt but flirting all the same. If they're very self-deprecating as they make jokes, then they're trying to bond. It's also the case when they do that while casting light on your own strengths. They want you to get closer and help them with whatever flaw they perceive.

Sign #17: It's all in the wrists. Do they have their right wrist in their left hand? Then they're probably sensually available. If it's their left wrist in their right hand, they're probably hostile. Be mindful of this one though, since it could be different depending on whether they're left or right-handed, or ambidextrous.

Three Steps to Successful Flirting

Understanding the way flirting works from personal experience will help you spot when someone else is trying to flirt with you. Things will probably happen in a certain way or order. Think of it as a script you follow. Say you're at the movies. You know that things go a certain way. First, you head over to the counter to get your ticket. Then you go get some popcorn and whatever else you want to snack on. Then you head to the cinema. The lights dim. The announcement asking you to turn off your cellphones comes on, and then the trailers start before you finally get to see the movie you paid for. This order of events helps to guide the way we behave and will also affect our expectations.

We also use scripts in our relationships, expecting certain behaviors to happen in a certain order. It's all usually subtle and nonverbal. For instance, you wouldn't beat your chest like a caveman and say, "Me. You. Sex. Now." Well, maybe you've roleplayed that, but that's not the point. It's probably more like you've both had a bath, one of you leans against the wall staring at the other a certain way, someone dims the lights, and then it's sexy time.

These patterns happen at the start of relationships too. Researchers Susan Fox and Timothy Perper have discovered there are three steps we all have to negotiate so our flirting can work out.

1. The approach. One person reaches out to the other. The other must respond positively, so the flirting can go on. If they don't, that's the end of that. Fun fact: Men don't like being approached from the front, and women don't like being approached from the side. For you to move from the approach to the next step, it's important that you smile genuinely and sincerely. How do you smile genuinely? Simple: *mean it.* Also, fake smiles are usually asymmetrical, delayed, and last longer than normal. Also, there are no crow's feet at the corners of the eyes. As you approach, you say hello, and you flash your eyebrow at the other person. The eyebrow flash is often an unconscious thing we all do when we're meeting someone we'd like to engage socially.

2. The swivel and synchronize. Say your approach was warmly received, then you'd need a conversation starter or an opening line to encourage back and forth banter. The last thing you want to say is bizarre, rude lines like, "Your place or mine?" "Is that your real hair?" "You remind me of someone I once loved." This stage is called swivel and synchronize because, after the approach, both parties turn so they can be face to face, and they match body movements, which means there's rapport going on. This is often a natural occurrence. Some people can mirror well, but look from their waist down at their lower legs and feet to figure out if they're interested in you. Remember, their knees and feet will be pointed your way if they want this to go on. This step also lets you look into their eyes, so you can tell by the dilation of their pupils if they're interested or not.

3. The touch. In this phase, one of you touches the other, and the other has to welcome the touch for the conversation to continue. Touch matters a lot for building rapport. At this stage, there's listening, talking, mutual sharing, and humor involved. According to Fox and Perper, women touch first, more often than not. That mutual sharing is also important, because the more people share with you, the more you like them, and the more they let you share with them, the more you like them. This is all backed by research. When at this stage, there's going to be humor. In opposite-sex flirtation, research has shown that interest in dating is more about the laughter that the woman gives, more so than the man.

Again, this is not some pick-up artist guide, so please don't run around trying to force these things to happen. The whole pick-up scene can be sleazy; avoid it if you're all about genuine connections.

You should have no problems figuring out who's flirting with you and who isn't now. Flirting can be fun, given the right conditions and with the right people, so, enjoy yourself responsibly.

Chapter Eleven: Identifying Mass Manipulation and Propaganda

We have the late, great intellectual Noam Chomsky to thank for first pointing out the strategies that the media uses to manipulate us. Ever since he wrote about them some three decades ago, the media has only developed even more ways to get to us. We now have Facebook, Instagram, Twitter, and so many other sources of information they can use to get us thinking in ways that benefit the viewpoint they hold. Sadly, the influence they wield isn't always for good.

Media Manipulation Tactics

Tactic #1: Create a diversion. This is the media's go-to ploy for manipulating its audience. They take important information you and I need to know and wedge it between a lot of inconsequential stories. It's even easier for them to do this now that we have the internet. (At least we have the option of simply filtering out parts that don't matter to us.)

Tactic #2: Blow a problem out of proportion. When they make a huge enough deal about something that probably isn't a huge deal (if we'd all stop to think about it), the media can get a rise out of society, fostering huge consequences. For instance, NASA put out an article in 2016, claiming that if there were any science at all to astrology, then the zodiac signs would have to keep changing their positions. A Libra would, at some point, be a Leo, a Scorpio, and so on. So, what did the popular Cosmopolitan magazine do? They put this claim out there like it was an actual scientific discovery, saying that 80 percent of people must switch zodiac signs. This went viral, forcing NASA to print a retraction.

Tactic #3: Poco a poco. In English: Bit-by-bit. When the media wants you to view things a certain way, it publishes its news materials bit by bit. For instance, if they wanted you to believe that the earth is flat, they wouldn't create a headline: Breaking News! Earth is Flat!" Not unless they don't feel like being in business any longer. Instead, they would start you off with a story about how some NASA satellite found a few flat planets just outside of our solar system. Then they would tell you that another version of Earth has been discovered in orbit, that it is flat, and has people on it. Finally, they'd wrap up with, "Hey, so, all the equipment we've been using to view the Earth from outer space all this time is super faulty and outdated. These newer telescopes now show that the Earth is flat." Yes, this is a ridiculous example, but believe it or not, the media has *that much* influence, and this strategy works. The media also uses this bit-by-bit strategy to create new habits or a "new normal" (sound familiar?). This is how they normalized smoking in the 20th century.

Tactic #4: Postponing. If the media wants you to have to make a tough decision, they will present it to you as "painful, but we don't have a choice." Next, they will let the audience know that they have to make a decision tomorrow, not this red-hot minute. It's easier to deal with sacrifices when you know they're coming, versus when they're staring you in the face.

Tactic #5: Kill them with kindness. You will find that advertisements geared toward children have a certain vibe about them. They use symbols, language, intonations, and arguments, all carefully crafted to make sure there is no criticism. You will also notice that brand slogans and ad copy use the imperative form, meaning they sound commanding like you don't have a choice. They also target you in the emotions by triggering basic feelings like fear, greed, the need to be a part of something, the need to feel a cut above others, and so on. This way, you find yourself making impulsive decisions, and you can't for the life of you figure out why.

Tactic #6: Emotions means thoughts off. A friend told me that in journalism class, they were literally taught, "Bad news is good news." That's the media. They are all about working up your emotions negatively so that you are blinded from the facts. You can't think objectively because they've done such a neat job of blocking out the rational part of you. Now, you see the version of reality they want you to see. This is the reason smear campaigns work. The next time you see someone being actively maligned by the media, hop on YouTube, and look for the speech taken out of context — preferably from a YouTube channel that is not mainstream media. You'd be surprised at what you notice. Information warfare is still a thing. Learn how to not get involved by turning off the TV, then asking yourself what emotions you feel, why you feel them, and about the facts.

Tactic #7: Un-inform sheeple. The media, along with the government, can actively manipulate the populace because most people do not get the mechanics of these manipulative techniques. Often, this is because of a lack of awareness. They are uneducated about the fact that no, the media is not your friend. It's serving an agenda, and that agenda probably doesn't serve you. According to Chomsky, the information that gets to the elite is a lot different from the information the "hoi polloi" gets. Thankfully, things have changed since his time, and now we can readily access alternate sources of information so we can judge the facts for ourselves. You don't have an excuse anymore to fall for the media's shenanigans.

Tactic #8: Feed them crap and make them love it. The media encourages people to stop thinking and to be more accepting of things that ordinarily, we would immediately dismiss as harmful or worthless. This is why we are inundated with so many movies, shows, sitcoms, tabloids, and all sorts of entertainment. It's not just for the harmless purpose of recreation, contrary to what you might assume. Entertainment is a great way to make sure that we're not looking at the problems looming over our shoulders, and by the time we do, it will be too late.

Tactic #9: The guilt trip. The strategy is simple. Make people assume they're the ones to blame for everything going wrong in the world. Let them blame themselves for things people did centuries ago. Make them blame themselves for the wars that governments spearheaded without their permission or support. There was a photo of a boy lying between his parents' graves that went viral in 2014. It was depicted as a picture from a war zone. In reality, the boy had taken the photo for a project showing love for his relatives. *Media at its finest.*

Tactic #10: Know them better than they know themselves. The media makes a point of learning all it can take about everyone, and in the process, they go overboard. Back in 2005, a British tabloid named News of the World was caught doing something so brazen and dastardly that it boggles the mind how they even thought they could get away with it for long. They were wiretapping politicians, celebrities, and members of the royal family. This was how they wrote so many "exclusive" articles, which pulled in a lot of readers. The tabloid was buried in lawsuits from ordinary people and celebrities, and after paying whopping amounts of compensation, they shut down.

Social Media Manipulates You Too

You might make a habit of checking all your feeds, but then, it would probably surprise you to learn that really, most posts do not accurately depict actual views held by actual humans. You know your cousin Betty is as real as they come and not some AI somewhere, but social media can un-inform you, misinform you, and mislead you. There is a lot of evidence that social media platforms make use of your data for other purposes, and this has been the practice even way before they officially came out with Facebook ads and Twitter ads. Bots and trolls are on these platforms, used solely to manipulate the way you think.

Tips for Dealing with Social Media

1. Do not trust them. You might be doing yourself a huge favor if you only followed the things that serve you and friends you do know. Facebook data was used in manipulating voters in the 2016 election; a scary thought. You would be better off not trusting these companies with your data unless they prove that you can. Be mindful of the content you like, or don't even bother with the "like" button. Whatever works for you. The less they know about you, the harder it will be for them to manipulate you.

2. Know your own perceptions. You don't want to be a part of the manipulative machine that is social media. There are a lot of biases we all have with our thinking, and these big tech companies know well how to exploit them. So, what should you do? Find all possible viewpoints on a subject. When you google something, don't just look at page one. Go all the way to page ten (or farther, if you can.) Better yet, after googling, run that search phrase through DuckDuckGo. You'll find that there's some interesting stuff you don't see on Google. Be quick to question any story you see out there, rather than "like and share" automatically.

3. Beware the power of bots. They are great at shifting public opinion to whatever the creator would prefer. MIT professor Tauhid Zaman demonstrated how Twitter activity surrounding politics would be a lot different if there were no bots on the platform. It's not about the number of bots. Their strength doesn't lie in numbers, but the number of posts they make.

4. Make a point of engaging with actual humans. In-person. You will feel a lot better about it. "Social" media isn't so social. It takes away from the benefits of having a real, live human to talk to. You feel even better when you connect with people right in front of you, not people looking at a screen like you are.

How Deep the Rabbit Hole Goes

Governments are actively making use of social media to manipulate the public. This begs the question, is democracy still a thing? Propaganda is nothing new. However, what makes social media worse is that it makes it easier to spread toxic messages on a worldwide scale. It doesn't help that now there are advanced methods to target specific users and to make the message even harder to get away from.

The University of Oxford's Computational Propaganda Research Projects says that shaping public opinion with automation, algorithms, and big data (computational propaganda) is now a part of our day-to-day life.

In its third yearly report, the project considered what it dubbed "cyber troop" activity, spanning 70 countries. In case you're wondering, cyber troops are what they sound like. It's the term used to describe actors representing the government or political parties, who manipulate public opinion, spread messages that are divisive, attack any political opponent, and harass all dissidents as well.

2017 saw a 150 percent surge in the number of countries with cyber troops launching these computational propaganda campaigns. The reason for this growth is that the masses have become a lot more sophisticated. They're better at being able to spot trolls and obvious manipulation. Another reason this is growing is there are countries only just getting the hang of social media, just now playing around with these computational propaganda tools.

Researchers found there were 56 countries with cyber troop campaigns on Facebook, which makes Facebook the king of the digital propaganda pile. Facebook works well because they've got the most users, and they can connect to not just you but your family, friend, and maybe in 2025, your neighbor's dog.

There is also cyber troop action on YouTube and Instagram, and WhatsApp. It is assumed that in the coming years, political communications will increase exponentially on these platforms. It doesn't help that it's not quite as easy to supervise video content as it is to supervise text, so the chances these fake videos can be taken down aren't looking too good.

When you're on social media, you have to know three kinds of fake accounts:

- Bots, which are very automated and designed to imitate human behavior on the internet. Often, these are used to drown out anyone who disagrees with a viewpoint or to amplify a narrative.
- Humans, who create more fake accounts than bots, and post tweets, comments, and also "slide into your DMs."
- Cyborgs, which are a blend of humans and bots.

There's one more fake account type: The stolen or hacked one. If an account has a high profile and a lot of followers, then they're extremely attractive to people looking to hijack them for their own purposes. They use these accounts to spread messages supporting the government's propaganda. Other times, these accounts are simply hacked to keep the owner from expressing their viewpoint.

Here are some scary stats: 87 percent of countries make use of accounts controlled by humans. 80 percent of them use bots. 11 percent of them make use of cyborgs. 7 percent of them use stolen or hacked accounts. 71 percent of all these accounts often spread propaganda that's pro-party or pro-government. 89 percent are set up to start smear campaigns or attack all opposition. 34 percent spread divisive messages to break people up into factions. 75 percent use media manipulation and disinformation to deceive users. 68 percent use trolls sponsored by the state to take shots at journalists, the opposition, or political dissidents. 73 percent flood social media with hashtags to amplify whatever messages they want.

22 Propaganda Techniques You Should Know

1. Stereotyping or name-calling: The idea or victim is given a terrible label, that is easy to remember and sounds pejorative. This way, the audience automatically rejects them without giving much thought to what the label represents. Examples of such labels: "Tree-hugger," "Nazi," "Special Interest Group," "Snowflake."

2. Glittering generality or virtue words: These are words chosen to trick the audience into accepting people or ideas without thinking much about the facts before them. Examples: "Organic," "Sustainable," "Scientific," "Natural," "Ecological."

3. Deification: This is making an idea or person into a god of sorts. They paint them as sacred, holy, or special and above all laws and conventions. When the opposite of this person or idea is presented, they are painted as blasphemous. Examples: "God-given right to..." "Gaia," "Mother Earth."

4. Transfer (Virtue or guilt by Association): A respected symbol that has authority, prestige, and is sanctioned is also used right along with a different argument or idea so it appears to be just as acceptable. Examples: University Seal, American Flag, Medical Association Symbol (or something akin to it).

5. Testimonial: A respected personality, or someone who is loathed, comes up to say that a product or an idea is good or bad. This way, the public doesn't look at the facts, but only focuses on the character of the person describing the idea or product.

6. Plain folks: This is a method of convincing the audience that an ideal is actually good because this same ideal is upheld by "other people just like you." They will use phrases like, "Most Americans...," "This is the will of the people," and so on.

7. Bandwagon: This is when the media wants you to accept what they're saying, by letting you know if you don't, you'll be missing out on some great benefits. This is used a lot in advertising. You'll hear phrases like, "Be the first among your friends," "Act NOW!" "Miss it, miss, out!" "This is the next big thing." Ask yourself if anyone else among your friends actually want sot to buy into the garbage you're being sold to snap out of that trance.

8. Artificial dichotomy: The media will try to get you to accept there are only two sides to a problem, and each side needs to be accurately represented for us all to make an honest evaluation. This dupes you into thinking there can be one only right way of looking at things. This works by simplifying reality, and then distorting it, to the media's advantage. Consider the controversy of "evolution" versus "intelligent design."

9. A hot potato: this is a question or a statement that is untrue and designed to elicit anger so that the opponent can be surprised and embarrassed. AN interviewer may leave discussion and veer off on a tangent to ask, "Do you still have issues with your husband?" or "When will you finally pay up all the taxes you're owing?" It doesn't matter that the questions are based on false premises. It does what it should do, which is to injure the reputation of the person being interviewed.

10. Ignoring the question or stalling: This gives the chance to escape a pointed question, or to get more time. Examples of phrases you'll hear are, "A fact-finding committee is investigating this matter..." "More research is required..." "I'm summoning a body to investigate this attack."

11. Least-of-evils: This is how they justify something that is unpopular and unpleasant. "War is terrible, but it is the price to pay for peace."

12. Scapegoat: This is used along with guilt-by-association to keep the public from scrutinizing the problem. It's about shifting the blame from one person or group to another, without really diving too deep into the gray areas of the problem. You'll hear statements like, "President Obama got us into this mess," or "Trump caused the drop in employment rates."

13. Cause and effect mismatch: This confuses the audience about the actual cause and effect in play. Most things are caused by more than one thing, and so it would be misleading to say, "Cancer is caused by bacteria," or "Cancer is caused by homosexuals in the United States."

14. Out of context or Distortion of data or Cherry picking or Card stacking: To convince the audience, the media will use selected information and not give the full story. They could put out a study that says diet sodas have been found to help with weight loss, but then you find they only studied people with an already active lifestyle, and the study was funded by Big Soda.

15. False cause or weak inference: This is when the media makes judgment but does not have enough evidence to pass that judgment. Also, the conclusion does not always tally with the evidence they do provide.

16. Faulty analogy: This is an overexaggerated comparison, like a slippery slope, where it is assumed that a slight movement one way will lead to a movement to the most extreme point that way. (Example: "Smoking marijuana leads to cocaine addiction!") They could say, "Bitcoin is surging the same way it did right before the great crash; therefore, we will see the bubble burst really soon!"

17. Misuse of statistics: They report average numbers, not the actual amount. They could say, "9 out of 10 doctors recommend...) without telling you that they literally only got that info from three out of four doctors they spoke to. They could also pull the trick of mixing proportional and absolute quantities, like this: "7,600 more rats died from drinking the agave nectar tea, while with others who stuck with chamomile, had a death rate of less than one percent."

They also use distorted graphs, where they might represent 7 out of 10 as 71.354 percent.

18. Fear: The media loves this one. Just tell the people that there's a threat and denounce all those not taking it seriously enough, as you accuse them of being unpatriotic and putting everyone else in danger. People will get scared, and they will fall in line.

19. Ad hominem attack (Deflection): Rather than attack the message, they attack the messenger.

20. Tu quoque attack: The media responds to their opponents by saying they are using a propaganda technique, or a logical fallacy, rather than focusing on their opponent's evidence and argument. They basically accuse the opponent of doing what they (the media) are actually doing.

21. Preemptive framing: They frame the issues the way they want people to perceive them. An example of framing would be, "The only reason we're having trouble with the economy is that the Dems were too busy doing anything but fixing it." Again, no effect has just one simple cause.

22. Diversion: Whenever something is threatening or embarrassing, the media comes up with a diversion. You may have noticed this during the Hong Kong riots, the media was eerily silent on the matter for a long time.

Chapter Twelve: Training Your Analytical Mind Daily

Let's talk about your analytical thinking skills. How are they? For some people, these skills come naturally. For others, they must work at them. You need to be driven and interested, displaying a lot of perseverance if you're going to acquire this skill. You're going to have to apply what you learn. That's what this chapter will help you with.

Why Analytical Thinking Skills Matter

They are critical in work and in your personal life. When you know how to think analytically, you can solve problems and spot solutions that people do not consider, even though they're as plain as the nose on your face.

With analytical thinking, you're able to see when emotions are causing everyone to go blind to the actual issues on the ground. You can also tell when you're not in the best position emotionally or mentally to decide. You do not allow yourself to be pressured into acting but think things through thoroughly. Often, this saves you money, time, and energy as you know the things essential for yourself and those around you at any given point in time.

When you must gather data, solve problems, or make sound decisions, you need to think analytically. When drawing conclusions from the data you've collected, you need to be analytical and efficient in thought. This skill is very desirable when managers seek who to hire, as it instantly makes you a good fit for the organization. To excel in life, give yourself the gift of sharpened analytical thinking skills. Here's how you can do that.

Seven Steps to Better Analytical Thinking

1. Observe everything. When you go for a walk, observe your environment and the people around you. When you're at work with colleagues, observe them. As you do, make sure to use all your senses, so that you have a truly immersive experience. What is it about what's going on that holds your attention now? Focus on those things. Make sure you keep your mind engaged.

2. Read more books. If you want to do well at thinking analytically, it is inevitable that you need to read more. This is how your mind stays sharp since you always keep it running and introduce it to new ideas. Don't just read willy-nilly; be proactive about creating a strategy for reading. Also, as you read, digest what you're reading. Ask yourself questions about it. Does it make sense? Read aloud if it helps you remain engaged with what you're reading. Go nuts with a highlighter. Try to predict where the book is headed.

3. Make a point of learning how things work. Don't just go looking for solutions to why your PC volume is way too loud after that last update. Dig deeper. Find out how things work, and you will be able to comprehend the process, which in turn will stimulate that analytical thinking muscle.

4. Make a habit of asking questions. When you get curious, you get smarter. Curiosity pushes you to make use of your cognitive functions, such as memory and attention. So ask some more questions, because this is how you get better retention, memory, and problem-solving skills. Do not ever let anyone make you feel

stupid for asking questions. It's a good and healthy thing to want to learn.

5. Play as many brain games as you can. To sharpen your analytical thinking skills, you should play games that work your brain. Try Sudoku, chess, crosswords, and puzzles. Download brain game apps that will keep you sharp. You can use the spare time you have in traffic or wherever to pay them and get better at thinking analytically. The great thing is that these games are fun, and so you should have no problem being motivated to play them.

6. Put your problem-solving skills to the test. Every problem has a solution. This should be your motto. So, always welcome the chance to solve a problem. Make a fun game of figuring out several different ways to fix one problem, and soon you'll find that you're the go-to person for solving issues. Where it's possible, don't just come up with the solutions, but test them as well. See which of them works the best, and then constantly ask yourself, "How could it be better?" You'd be surprised to find that there is really no end to improvement if you put your mind to it.

7. Consider your decisions carefully. In life, we have to make decisions, whether it's quitting our job to get started on the thing we want to do the most, or it's figuring out if this is the person you want to spend the rest of your life with. You should make a point of thinking long and hard about your decisions, making sure that they are, in fact, rational. Think through the pluses and the minuses, the pros, and the cons. Where you can get it, seek expert opinions on the matter. Don't be afraid of doing research, by which I mean extensive research, not just a Google search where you content yourself with page-one answers. Also, ask yourself if the solution you've come up with is the absolute best one. Don't be afraid to listen to your inner critic, because it just could lead you to an even better solution than you already have. It's okay to take a little more time to rethink your stances on issues before you finally decide.

When it comes down to it, analytical thinking is a skill, and like all skills, the only way you do better at them is to practice and apply what you learn each day. You want to make sure that you mine the gold from every experience that you encounter.

Keep practicing. At first, it will feel like the most unnatural thing in the world. You might be tempted to beat yourself up because you feel you're no good at this. Don't give in to that feeling. Think of it like going to the gym. You're not going to bench press 34 reps of 320 pounds in a day just because you walked in, especially not if you haven't been training your muscles. In due time, you will get better.

When you do, you will find that you can read people easily, without really putting much effort into it. Your mind and your gut will align, each sense sharpening the other so that you have a better read on people. Your relationships will improve, you'll do better at work, and never again will you find yourself stuck with another person's toxic behavior without knowing how to handle yourself every moment.

Printed in Great Britain
by Amazon

19613483R00129